SUB POP CULT

SUB POP CULT

SUB POP CULT

THE NEW SYMPHONIC REITERATION

MICHAEL McGRUTHER

HOSEL & FERRULE BOOKS

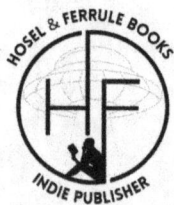

HOSEL & FERRULE BOOKS

INDIE PUBLISHER

This book is a reiteration of the SubPopCult Podcast.

Copyright © 2022 by Michael McGruther

All rights reserved.

———

www.hoselbooks.com
www.subpopcult.com

For Artists on the Right
Who Fight The Good Fight

"It's the culture, stupid."

— MICHAEL MCGRUTHER

INTRODUCTION

Culture creates the national narrative and the national narrative enables our political reality. America is more divided than ever before and it's not an accident and it's not going to magically mend itself. The outrageous and disingenuous political divide is too profitable for the multinational corporations that produce our junk food snacks and distribute our junk food pop culture. Both kill you over time and there's no reason to keep consuming them. Together we can establish a richer, truly organic *Sub Pop Culture* that runs parallel to the corporate cookie cutter media offerings. Let them have the high ground, we'll take the low ground and start anew —one story at a time, one poem at a time, one song at a time, one piece of art at a time. Valuing and supporting truly indie work that edifies what's good and true about American life will fix our problems faster than any slick politician with good slogans and media adoration. We must turn to each other and establish a counter-culture community of creators and entertainers that can serve the audience that was left behind—Mr. and Mrs. John Doe. We The People are now the counter-culture in a world of globalist storytelling and values. Ghost the mainstream corporate culture and spend time building the new one, or patronizing it's independent creators and keep your entertainment money away from the mega-corps that see you as data on a spreadsheet and not a human being with an eye for beauty.

SUB POP CULT

L ife in America is messed up right now, and I understand how we got here. I know there's been brilliant political minds doing deep dives and writing endless amounts of news articles about why they think it's happened, why we're in the bitterly divided situation we're in. But really, there's only one reason we're in the situation we're in and it's the all important C word—CULTURE.

The culture is cultivated by the media. The media uses narrative to instill qualities in the audience that increase its ability to make money from them. The narrative is the common story that we all get from the media we consume. It's what we get from pop culture, from movies, television, books, news broadcasts, memes, everything. All of that together. You throw it all in a pot and mix it around. That's the culture. And if it tastes like poison right now, there's a reason for it. It's designed to. Why would anyone take the culture into such a disastrous intersection of right versus left, amplified by the media, amplified by the stories told in pop culture that make enemies out of everybody? There's a very simple answer to this, and it's not very pleasant to understand. The American audience used to represent the largest audience with disposable income in the world. And if you wanted to be famous or become a rock star, you had to come to America to be seen on the big stage. The Beatles weren't famous because they came from England, they became famous in America because America has always served as the big giant world stage where legends are made and problems get worked out. People rise from nowhere and they become something that a lot of us know. Businesses get built from people tinkering in garages, social movements, things like that. They have all come from the bottom up and defined the reality from there. The problem now, is the people who run the culture started their revolution in the 1960s by just ripping it away from the Greatest generation, which came of age truly understanding that the world could end after nuclear bombs were dropped on Japan. A lot of huge, devastating human history happened that really gave the general public a sense that we can all die in an instant. And so in the 1950s, for that reason, a priority was put on kindness––legitimate kindness, not fake kindness, but actual encouraging kindness in stories, in movies that build up good qualities in people, so we could avoid repeating what happened in World War Two. And it was really successful at first, but like any social engineering it alienated a lot of people in public, and those folks now are the ones who are alienating and ignoring the same folks who didn't consider them long ago. Neat how that works, right? It's just this big giant cycle of back and forth. That's why I think it's important that we kick off the right wing 1960s through a new artist driven approach to small government and the preservation of liberty through storytelling and art.

Look at all the the civil rights movements that started in that era. You have the Stonewall riots in the 1960s, where the police and the gay community had a violent riot in Greenwich Village over the freedom to even hang out in a gay bar. Folks start their revolutions violently. Then they acquire power, and then they do every single thing they can to not let anyone take it from them, except the greatest generation. The Greatest generation didn't do that. The Greatest generation passed the baton because they knew that it was the right thing to do. But the folks from the 60's generation who got control of the baton, let's say the baby boomers at large, they refused to pass the baton to the folks that followed them. As a matter of fact, my generation, Generation X, is the smallest generation. I'm not going to get too political about specific issues, but the only reason Generation X is so small, is pretty sad. We come right after Roe versus Wade was made into law, and the folks that gave birth to my generation aborted half of us, and they replaced their children with an increasing amount of nice things and power and money. And the general public who are way, way, way, way downstream follow the lead of their cultural ambassadors who sell them a lifestyle disguised as storytelling. That's the power that only comes through culture.

We have this inconsequential generation that they literally labeled X and then X'd our political impact out. Get-X was followed by generations that could be manipulated and basically controlled through this new cultural power, now wholly owned by a group we shall call the Washington and Wilshire Nexus. It's a group of like minded very powerful people with tremendous amounts of money and tremendous amounts of ability that are steering this ship in the direction it's going in, and it's all to prevent you from ever getting your hands on the wheel. The reason you can't get your hands on the wheel is also pretty simple. It's because the globalists in our own government and around the world have all worked together to bring China online, starting with being brought into the World Trade Organization. And over time, the Chinese communist government has established a system in their country that is sort of glowingly referred to as red capitalism by some people on the left in American politics. But take that and set it aside, what they really achieved is they brought a middle class online bigger than any middle class in the world, where all things will be decided in the culture by this giant middle class. You no longer come to America and go to Hollywood to star in a feature film and the American audience chooses you as a role model and a celebrity because they love your work and they love what you're all about. Now you go to different lands and you cater to different views and different sets of realities, because that's where the disposable income is now. That disposable income that all these folks have to spend on entertainment puts them in the driver's seat at companies, virtually, that want to cater to audiences. That is why we, as Americans, are being attacked by our brands, attacked by our media, divided by Hollywood and ridiculed by anybody that has a vested interest in profiting from the world's largest middle class: the Chinese people. The Communists have reversed the game table and turned the whole thing around so that there is no more center of gravity in America. There is no more center of gravity in Hollywood. It has all been displaced, simply so these bastards can make more money. So now that I've told you the ugly truth, forget all the small little battles that are rained down on you daily in the media you consume. (I'm going to coin a phrase—*trickle down bullshit*.) They bullshit at the top. They trickle it down. And then what we do is we sit around and fight over their bullshit. They want you to look at their juxtapositions. *This guy said this and this happened to him. How come the same thing didn't happen to the other guy when he said the same thing?* It's all the same con against reasonable thinking so let's get past it. Let's admit that the left won the culture war, and let's admit and understand that they did it just to enrich themselves. And let's also admit that there is no way back into the mainstream culture for the right. And that's fine with me because I'm here to help encourage you to build a new culture. I'm here to preach a kind of right wing apologetics about why it's important to even have a culture that edifies good qualities in people.

So here's the recipe to undo the inversion Here's the basic Sub Pop Cult manifesto: Culture works like a symphony. You get all kinds of people saying the same thing because reiteration is an important way to establish reality and change minds. And so if you if you pay attention to the mainstream media, it reiterates reiterates, reiterates everything they want you to know, which is kind of why Trump, as president, always reiterated "fake news" just to make you really, really get that sunk into your head. Performing the reiteration is a nice high paying job. If you're welcome into the club, you can make lots of money reiterating whatever it is that benefits the folks who are in charge. But if you want to reiterate things that make your life better, make your community better, make your interactions with folks who disagree with you better, well, that's going to take a good decade of indie storytelling where we on the right become like the off-off-Broadway storytellers, we become the underground, the cool, edgy, fun, new way to do things with a new mindset about American life, and we do it by not trying to get rich. We have to do it by carving out for ourselves within this culture (if you're a creator) small, little niche audiences. If you can make $50,000 a year and you're living in Kansas and you've got your own streaming TV show, something that you're doing that is not meant to be totally serious, but you're just a dabbler. But if you've monetized that dabbling and you're putting the right message into your material, the American audience is going to respond as soon as they start to collectively understand that we have to look to each other for the truth, and we can't look to the media companies which always attach a paycheck to what the truth is going to be that day. So we have to create our own independent symphony and that's going to take millions of creators not trying to get 10 million dollar deals from Sony or Warner Brothers, but trying to make $50000 or $100000 selling their self-published books, their independent music, poetry, TV shows. I admire James O'Keefe. I think he's an incredible success, and it's not because he's always pulling a fast one and getting the left to fall on its own sword. It's because James O'Keefe took basically a great TV show like 20/20, and he made it all his own. He is a real journalist with a real TV show. I think of James O'Keefe as a show host I want to watch. I want to watch the Project Veritas show. It's my attempt to understand things in a more clear way, and I like the journalistic work that they do, and I love how their whole agenda is just being journalists and getting you to really have a different perspective on things. So look at him as a business role model. What show can you create? What program can you unpack and reinvent right in your garage or backyard?

This is my prediction. The next big movie star in America. The next big, famous personality is going to be some guy in Iowa, Kansas, wherever—some John Wayne type who makes his own movies. Who does it all out of his garage and in those movies he edifies the right values in the right things, and he monetizes that and he becomes our chosen cultural representative. He becomes our new John Wayne. Pop culture needs these touchstone personalities to kind of bump us forward, lead us forward. And if we're being led astray by bad shepherds who are all contaminated by corporatism, we need to identify new ones. We need to start following and paying for their work and supporting them. And when we do that, we will establish a new symphonic reality of reiteration that will be the true culture because it will be made by the people and it will be distributed by the people and it will be purchased by the people and we will go around all of the media companies. Of course, you have to access certain things to publish a book and sell it to somebody, but you can do that and you're not going to get canceled. Trust me, you're not going to get canceled. These companies benefit from this lower tier production and distribution of independent work. Do it but understand you're also not going to get rich. This is where we're at. We're not in the get rich chapter of the new reiteration. We're in the get going chapter and we're all vaudeville entertainers now.

ANOTHER TIME FOR
CHOOSING

I decided that it was time to start explaining to people what I know about the political game behind the scenes, which is known as the right wing movement to save the culture. I was disappointed to learn that it was fake, but I was determined to tell you or to at least show you what I know about this cottage industry of never fixing problems, but always making money talking about fixing the problems. It's a disgrace and we've let it go on for too long. And so I started the SubPopCult podcast with that purpose in mind and now this book. I'm here to liberate your mind from the distractions that prevent you from creating things with your God given talents that make the world yours instead of corporations. Even if you're not a creator but still a participant in the culture and you're looking for ways to engage with people who are planting the seeds that become the beautiful trees to provide shade for all of us all—this grassroots culture movement is also about that. It's about discovering new talent, exposing their work and celebrating what's good while sharing it with an audience. Realize that you must look here to your fellow Americans who are independent creators if you want to restore American culture. It's the only way to get off of the corporate storytelling agenda. The corporations will come and they will take the most talented people that we find here, and they will draw them into the system, pay them a lot of money, do their top down big, bloated, heavy business model, and that's OK with me.

What needs to happen is that a Sub Pop Culture becomes the underground network of like minded individuals creating art, and the only like minded quality that is required here is individuality and thinking for yourself, creating on your own terms. Going against the corporate worldview is critical because it co-opted every part of American life and now divides us as part of its business plan. We need to subversively separate culture and storytelling from their business model, which is about making you fall madly in love with products and ideals which are not really your own, instead of falling in love with liberty, justice for all the American way—those qualities that we so badly need in our culture because it truly is our culture and it's easily found in the world of independent creators that are trying to make a piece of storytelling for you or a piece of art for you. On the purist level, they're not the folks making $10 million sponsored by Coca-Cola, sponsored by Folger's crystals, or whatever the Hell corporation is behind the advertising push for whatever show—these people operate at a true level, and that true level will always reflect the qualities that we want in our culture because they're necessary to operate at that true level. And that's where the majority of the people who are young and talented find themselves right now. The system is so top heavy making the resources so limited. Identity politics is poisonous. Woke culture is repulsive. So everybody who has an untouched mind but is just an inventive kid living in another state somewhere far from power who wants to tell stories—all of these people are going to tell you the truth about what it's like to be an American in the United States of America in the year 2022.

This really, truly is another time of choosing. It's a different kind of choice. The choice is this: are we going to be unpaid agents of corporations, acting as their mini advertisers, reiterating slogans and things that push products and wealth into the pockets of a few people? Or are we going to choose to be Americans who create new things, create new stories, create new ways of rediscovering our common ground, our vast common ground, the ground that was fought and died for to preserve our rights, the rights that we are going to let slip away if we make the wrong choice? The rights that empower us to find and seek one out and to team up and make things, and when I say things, I really mean the world because we are about to remake the entire world, and it starts right here in the United States between the little people but also depends on independent creators because all power comes from narrative. Don't listen to the cheerleaders on the fake right who suddenly want to be your best friends in loss. Stay the course. Stay true. Be neither right nor left. Befuddle the system's entire business plan by being wishy washy and seeing good things on both sides so we can neutralize the ability to divide us against one another so that we only empower those who have the dividing rods

I like what we got here and I know you do too. It's very important that we all focus on how easily it can slip away, how easily our fellow Americans can be manipulated into rooting for this great country of unique people and all of its blessings to be fully converted into a cold and uncaring system that relies exclusively on data and technology. Computers that run the world have taken over the government. An ingenious system that was established by the people for the people and of the people has been completely replaced by a system that is by the data for the data and of the system. The system requires your data but the system is quickly requiring less and less administrators at the same time. Power is becoming dangerously consolidated in the United States of America. It is up to all of us individual American citizens to recognize which team we're on. We're on Team Citizen. The system is not supposed to work against us, it's not supposed to divide us, and it's certainly not supposed to keep us down. Maybe we've all tasted enough of the bad medicine to finally unite around this ideal that the system has no heartbeat. We the People do. And it's time to move together and grow together and create together and love together. The blessing that we have on this planet, which is called the United States of America, the land of the free and the home of the brave. Let's keep it that way.

DISUNITY

T he Sub Pop Cult revolution is about understanding the rules of the game once and for all. Finding out who's motivated by what incentive. Finding out who provides the incentive. Learning that this whole entire political narrative game is about keeping all of the people divided so that the corporations increase their profits, and at the end of the day, decrease unity among the American public.

Why would anyone want to create disunity in the American public? It's an obvious answer—to weaken the United States of America. You know the phrase united we stand, divided we fall. We are divided. We're bitterly divided. And we're falling because of it. There's two mindsets that operate in this country, it doesn't matter where you live, there's the East Coast mindset and there's the West Coast mindset. It was best described to me, and I'm a guy who's lived in both places, as hustlers and con men. Hustlers are trying to really make something out of their life. They're hustling and get up early. They do the hard work. They're always at the font of the line trying to sell their product. They're the guy or the gal whose hustle is the reason for their success and everyone sees it. Hustle is not a shadow dance and it's really something that is embedded throughout the East Coast, north to south but really personified in New York City, the city that never sleeps. Hustle is an American quality that began here on the East Coast and is embedded in the way that people live their lives. They hustle. Then there's con men. Con men all come from the West Coast mindset. People who moved out to the West built a world of their own, created a fantasy storytelling world and use that fantasy storytelling world to change the way the public views itself through storytelling, persuasion and propaganda. What you find out after watching it, studying it, participating in it—is that it's a big con. It's not a hustle, it's a con. And the result of a con is a lot different than the result of a hustle. When somebody hustles you, they got a couple of your dollars. When somebody cons you, they have everything that was yours, including the things that you didn't even know were yours. That's what happened with the media. The media conned the American people out of their freedom and think they are entitled to program the global audience as its corporate culture leaders, but they're not. Right now, the movie business, the television business in the United States is on life support and in international markets, China squeezes Hollywood out on the thinnest of margins. But we all knew they were going to do it. So Hollywood is being squeezed. The culture is at this breaking point, and we're starting to see that we're all in different fish tanks and we got put here by a tyranny of divisive storytelling. That's what is really eating this country alive, because we take in divisive storytelling and then we broadcast it back to one another in a kind of cage match death fight against unity. It doesn't help anything. It just helps the people who want to destroy us. So we have to break the fish tank. We have to stop swimming in our own little circles of influence and knowledge and really get into the ocean of life together. Because I'll tell you something, friends, the United States of America hasn't lost its way. The stories being told about us are stories aiming to divide us and make some of the weak minded folks within our society believe that we have fallen. We don't really have all the anxiety, all the evil, all the division like you see on social media. It exists in a vapor of story that is not out your front door.

THE NIGHTMARE
ENDS NOW

The erasing of American history from our collective subconscious is happening at a record pace while most of the monetized political personalities that you follow on social media (on the right) are warning about an impending move to a gulag. Well, I've got very bad news. The gulag exists, you're already in it, and it's run and operated by the corporate left and their unintentional minions on the right keep it alive as part of their business model. There's an unspoken power-share that happens in political punditry and when you begin to accept it—is when you begin to see the true reasons we on the right are always coming up short for power. If you're an American with classic values, you belong in the gulag, and the only way out of the gulag is to become a performer for the system, who then keeps other classic value Americans gulag'd so they never break out and change the culture. (Where all power comes from.) Let's examine this phenomenon because it is time for Republicans to eat the Pundicrats.

Pundicrats are what I call monetized political pundits on the right. They are the personalities that are the rich and famous on the right. We the artists need to have the pundits behind us, not in front of us. Every bestseller, every person who's made a movie that's purely political, every personality that has a million plus followers and the reach to be able to sell stupid political merch—all of them are Pundicrats first and foremost. None of them are attempting to create or promote culture. This is backwards. This is wrong. And it's got to end right now.

Here's the secret that someone can only tell you who's been inside the heart of fame-seeking darkness. The secret is that everybody wants to be famous. Period. Admit it. Be realistic. You want to be famous too. When I got into show business, I wanted to be famous. That's in the back of my mind the whole time. I was the kid who needed the attention in school, and the class clown is a natural fit to go and seek fame. But then there's the kids who don't have the ability to perform, who don't have the ability to create anything that has heart. But they're clever and data driven. And so they understand how they can get involved in show biz through political punditry, and what they ended up doing is filling a void that was created by people like myself. I sacrificed a screenwriting career and relationships with people to fight for cancelled and blacklisted talent on the right because I was already one of the victims of the sweeping away of undesirables. The good fight turned out to be a scam. We all know now that there was nothing that was ever going to change about the culture that enables the left to dominate the right in media. There was never going to be people who got together and built a studio and made entertainment that captured the American audience. All of the right wing startups are not for that purpose. The purpose was the establishing of a mental gulag/marketplace and keeping us conservative minded artists in it. Nothing disgusts me more, so let's examine this dynamic in a timetable of events that I had a front row seat to—that many of you did not. Right before Obama was elected president, conservative minded artists gathered in California and started a club call

Friends of Abe. It attracted all of the people who were disenfranchised by the business or blacklisted (like myself) and suddenly there was a movement to organize and right the wrongs and restore balance to the great storytelling business. It was well run and quickly grew its numbers. And so thousands of us would get together and have, basically, kumbaya meetings where we were trying to be inspired to take over the culture by retaking Hollywood over time. All of the parties and "secret meetings" led to nothing, really. It was just the collection of all the folks that might be a danger to the system who were now organized into one group but made completely ineffective by subversive elements that came in and dismantled the whole movement as a side effect of their own battle to rule the new conservative media fiefdom.

A lot of us gave up careers. A lot of us gave up relationships. A lot of us did the right thing, and we held true to the values that we know are the right values that belong in popular entertainment. And we had our careers ruined. Run into the ground. *You're not going to work here anymore. Don't call us. We'll call you* for lots and lots of people. Very successful people. People who have children, people who have mortgages, people who built lives and had it turned off in an instant. The "cancel culture" you're seeing now on a large scale happened 15 to 16 years ago to many of us who were already in the business and finding out before the public that conservatives were not welcome anymore.

And then there's a void.

An eight year void where Obama is president and the FOA movement is wishy washy and it doesn't really know what it's doing and all the folks who got cut away and thrown in the trash, myself included, we just kind of floated off into the what the hell, what's going on here wind? Then the political narrative experts and their minions and all the fake hustlers who sell us bullshit stories started The Donald Trump Show and The Donald Trump Show was damn good. All of us loved it because this guy was going to aggressively attack the system. There was no reason not to support Donald Trump if you were somebody who knew that politics was narrative. And President Trump represented the greatest plot twist to the left's storytelling that we had seen in a long time, and it was beautiful. But new personalities started to emerge that were never around when this movement started and suddenly were front and center. Suddenly they had the ear of the organized right wing artist base, telling us how this was all going to play out to win the culture war. Even though not one of them were there during the early years of conservative blacklisting or the formation of the movement that put wind in Donald Trump's sails in the first place. He wouldn't have had that otherwise. He wouldn't have had any of the support if the mission of retaking Hollywood didn't fall away first, which makes me angry that the culture was completely abandoned and that the people who became the face of the culture war are all frauds—all pundits, all folks who sell you political narrative 24/7 and secretly every single one of them wants to be a filmmaker. Every single one of them wants to be an actor. Every single one of them would rather be doing something else, but this was the way in so they took the door and they went in, and now they're doing the system's bidding, which is keeping you the conservative artist down. Keeping you celebrating their brilliant punditry, keeping you paying attention to what they're doing because they're getting the little bit of fame carved out of the system, the only way they know how, the only way they're capable of. They do that and then we cheer them on. Well, my friends, I've been in the cheering section of this charade for two administrations now. For a total of 12 years, I've seen the system completely play the artists on the right. The artists on the left get something for their dedication and commitment to the culture. Their politicians, believe it or not, are beholden to them. We on the right are so lost that we are defined by Jack Posobiec, Ian Miles Chong or Mike Cernovich instead of artists? These people are all characters/influencers. They're not the movement. They didn't even start the movement. They came in and took advantage of a gulag that they knew already existed and monetized it for themselves. I'm trying to break you out, friends. I'm trying to get you free. I'm trying to release you from the bullshit because the only reason we're living in the world we're in, is because it was imagined by others and we didn't release our art. We waited. We followed pundits.

Being victimized is exactly the way to get attention. Well, guess what conservative artists? You're the victims of the biggest con of them all. It's called the right wing movement that's going to change the culture. And the only guy that's really going to help you change the culture is your fellow artists like myself. I bought all the Mark Levin books. I've bought the Ann Coulter books. I forwarded all the articles I've retweeted and shared all the things that were never about the culture, but always complained about what's wrong. I'm not doing it anymore. I'm off that losing game play. It doesn't benefit me and it doesn't benefit you. It is long past time to end this charade of right wing punditry. If you follow me on social media, you know that I call right wing punditry a cottage industry because I recognize it for what it really is. They see that a large group of people have been organized and that they are not welcomed into the mainstream narrative. So you just grift and sell them political products. That's how cold these people are. That's how they think. They want to take advantage of you because they know how to take advantage of you, and it's been going on for decades in a row. We can't do this anymore. You can't tune in to that stuff and expect anything to ever change in politics. You have to tune out and you have to drop in—by drop in, I'm saying you need to drop in to what I'm doing focusing on and demanding a voice in the culture. You need to join me because there's only one way to succeed at this, and there's a reason Andrew failed. I saw it with my own eyes.

Fame got Andrew Breitbart, it took him off mission —you have to completely reject fame to do this ground level work. You have to completely reject amassing personal wealth too because the only way that the left's power works is they make you famous and rich so that they can dramatically tear you down. What I want you to do is join me in frenetically creating indie art that aims to unite Americans because there is common ground with the creators on the left. There truly is, because at the end of the day, people who are artists cannot separate that part of their personality from who they are. That's how we experience life. We become reflectors of the things that we experience, and you see that in our art. There are a lot of people on the left that are intentionally misleading the entire culture because they have the main stage and it's very profitable for them. We won't let that happen for much longer if we get on board with the real focused effort of becoming a very potent artistic community. Let me tell you a little story about a lunch I had years ago before everything that I'm telling you was clear to the general public. I was with the director of My Dog, Skip. His name is Jay Russell. We were at a very trendy Mexican restaurant in Los Feliz. It's one of those places where nearly every table has a recognizable face, having lunch with a recognizable name. The only dude I saw alone that day was Will Wheaton. He sat and chewed and stared off into space like he was watching episodes of The Honeymooners on the television in his imagination. That's one of the fun things about being involved in the movie business is you go around and you do your daily work and you run into all these characters that you know from entertainment.

That's part of the charm. The bitter narrative at the time of Republican versus Democrat was really not fully emerged. The blacklisting had been going on quietly by uncovering what you really believe in meetings that had nothing to do with the story, but everything to do with your political views. This was just starting to become a regular thing and I was sitting at this lunch with Jay figuring out, you know, where the future is going and feeling some opposition to the values of the folks that I was spending a lot of time with. So I, an amoral atheist screenwriter, was making an argument for morality. Jay rolled his eyes and he looked at me point blank and said *the right doesn't own the patent on morality.* He was right and that's why I want you to know this truth and take it right into your heart and into your mind and use it as a prism to forever create—the left does not own the patent on art. They're just the ones who created a culture around daring to create with wild abandon and no cares in the world. When we start doing that we will change the culture. Or you can stay tuned in to the political grifters and the persuasion experts, and you can keep buying their books and reiterating their reactions, and when you really find out how awful society can be, you can use those books as firewood to warm your home. Or you can feast right now and eat the Punditcrats and then create the new world.

Let's make artistic freedom great again. Let's take every slogan and turn it into our favor. Let's take every false story and throw it right in the circular filing cabinet. And let's take each other's art and share it among ourselves and share it among our family and friends. And let's restore the American culture that we all know and love—the true story of who we are. Let's never forget that the winners not only write the history books, but they create the culture. And I don't know about you, but I'm sick and tired of helping pundits be winners in exchange for no culture and less freedom.

THE SCAM

It's something we all watch unfold on social media across all platforms by the folks who comprise the political narrative personalities on the right that I call "Pundicrats." They are a perfect example of playing the game and playing the game to win. The problem is they're playing the game to win against their fellow conservatives who are desperate to be represented in culture and politics. That's the issue, so what I try to do here at Sub Pop Culture is I want to inspire you to be in competition with the folks who fooled you into not competing with them in the first place. There is a big prize that can be won. And that big prize can and should be divided among many, many, many, many millions of creators instead of consolidated among a small group who keep most of the treasure and behave exactly like the people in power on the left that they want to become. One tried and true way they secure their future is by distracting you from your own goals by inspiring you to participate in trivial games like "owning the libs." Owning the libs is essentially the conservative version of virtue signaling. Think about it, every side of the left has an absolute equal opposite on the right and they both serve the same purpose. It's all a big show. It's all a big distraction. I said in my very first podcast episode that we have to establish a new symphonic reality of reiteration to overcome this assault on unity and focus. Reiteration is the constant repeating of the same talking points so that it sinks in and becomes accepted truth. The paid and monetized indie pundits are very clever at the persuasion game, and they all reiterate one another so that it becomes a symphony. It doesn't matter who you look at, who you see, whether it's Ben Shapiro or Candace Owens or Matt Walsh. They're all excellent at playing this game of putting something inflammatory out there that draws attention to their organization, to themselves, and everybody fights over that ridiculous thing they placed before you. This is the game I've been telling you about, and I don't mind if they play but I'm interested in creating competition so that they can't do to the grassroots artist right exactly what the left did to the right, to your own people, because that's what these types of political character actors are doing. And the reason it's intolerable is this just isn't where the future is going, the future is not about consolidating power into the hands of the same few people who've been running things as a way to empower themselves. It's about the empowerment of everybody because now the tools exists to do so.

Social media is used by Pundicrats to maintain a world of distance that enables people to hide behind a mask and fight each other in insult theater. And so that's why it's constantly used. That's why *owning the libs* is a recurring theme on the right. It's pushing that button inside you that gets off on the quick little cheap win of getting one over on the other guy. Getting one over and the other guy is fine. I've said it bunches of times on my podcast. I can be as sarcastic as anybody, but I try to tamper down that part of my personality and I try to reel it in now because I recognize what I'm trying to have you understand with me is that we have a much bigger problem here. We have our country being gamed with finances that come from outside of our country and people who are organized outside of our country. They come in and find business partners and together they create "culture" institutions that are directed towards commerce on the surface—yes, they would like to make money—but if you look closer, it's just more political programing that is always supposed to get you into some extreme ideological political gulag, whether it's on the right or the left, the foreign investors want you so dialed in to one side or the other so that the middle ground is theirs to monetize and profit off of forever.

That's the scam, we can't tolerate it, we can't accept it and it's unnecessary. The only way that we get over it, is if we keep reminding ourselves, which is what I'm doing right now with this book, that it is a con from the left and the left created the fake right and the fake right does everything in its power to prevent you from going after your dreams or even thinking they're possible when really all it takes is a little bit of organization and a new reiteration. There should be 25 Real Daily Wires competing in the United States of America. There should be 25 Media Matters for America. There should be 50 Breitbarts. There should be a million little creators making everything, because you know what? The top down heavy system, that one that is desperately trying to prevent you from seeing that its corrupted to death—is dead. The system died for the same exact reason that a human diminishes their connection to the mysteries of life and dies spiritually—the system died by becoming too infected with greedy and worldly game players who knowingly anticipate that one story runs its course and a new story must be written, a new story must be told and so the same players who have been in power for most of my life tried to tell that story without any competition. One way you can know it was all a scam is by looking at what is reiterated in the story. Reiteration really does make the reality and therefore, the accepted truth in the minds of the casual observer audience that accepts any story on the surface and never looks beneath it or tries to see the innuendo or the metaphor in creative writing. There's a rule that says when you want to tell the audience something important you have to tell them three different ways. First, you hit the nail right on the head and you establish what it is you're trying to communicate to the audience. The second time, it's a little bit more abstract. Maybe it's told in a juxtaposition of things that the characters are dealing with. And the third time you tell them, you usually choose some kind of metaphor that strengthens the same message. So telling the audience things three times three different ways (but it's the same essential message) is one of the keys to reiterating into reality the same narrative across the board. It's why so many people involved in the political reiteration business don't really know what they're doing.

A meme is just a small, compacted idea, easily understood, that is shared among the social media public. That was the original definition of a meme, in not so many words. It was a social norm that got spread virally by people. And so, taking characteristics and turning them into little bitter angry images that tell you why you shouldn't be a "Chad" or why you shouldn't be this or that or mocking something trivial like clothing choices, is one of the reiterations of the overall punditry driven media on the right. And because of that, it sticks and it's fun and it turns into a game. And the sharing of those memes is the public constantly reiterating the secret messages, the secret division, (the obvious division to some) that is embedded in all of these memes. So not only in the modern era has the corrupt storytelling industry, the corporate storytelling industry, figured out how to reiterate things three different ways from what it really is, but also how to create mini reiterators out of everybody. I mean, that's that's part of the social media mojo is to have tweets that are liked millions of times or shared hundreds of thousands of times or whatever. That's how we've been trained to measure success, by how many people are reiterating what you're saying. So let's reiterate what I'm saying, because what I'm saying is to reiterate your own independence, to reiterate only things that encourage everybody to go their own way because going your own way is not separating from the pack and being selfish, going your own way is establishing more social norms that break us off of the disingenuous groupthink, break us off of the tribal attitudes that we've all been trapped in. There is no tribe in the United States that can supersede the individual and the individual's personal liberty. So we must reiterate things that edify and deepen our commitment to personal liberty being central to everything that we do as creators. It's vitally important. It doesn't mean that you cannot have stories about your LGBTQ lifestyle, it doesn't mean that you can't have content and entertainment that is focused around one specific thing that that you're into. Let's just use the gay community as an example because they've been in the center of the spotlight for a very long time now. It means that you can take that desire for equality and you can spin it two ways in storytelling. You can turn it into an us versus them narrative and therefore anyone can be made into the enemy and they must be cancelled. But that just serves the media. Or you can reiterate the need for personal liberty and the desire to live and let live where you will find yourself right back at this truth, which is the media's reiteration and all of their fake opposition are there to prevent you and I from ever really coalescing around the truth that we can fix all of these divisions when we dare to remember who we are.

"The narrative" is all about keeping us bitterly divided and locked in these little meme war thought camps and little hideouts of like minded people. When the real, like-minded quality of all Americans is that you live your life and I live mine and where we meet in the middle, we have a common ground and that common ground is called kindness.

So while the left is always pushing for kindness, kindness, kindness, that's all I experience in life. I've been all over this nation and I've never really encountered the level of anger and bitterness in my own people, in my own daily life. I only see it on television. Think about your own experiences as you go about your day.

THE COWARDS

Politics for the left is a way to beat the right into fighting things that are not real. Politics for the right is a way to monetize the reactions to the fake politics of the left. Put the two together, and you have both reasons that the United States of America is so divided. It's because of the politics. We're hooked, we can't get off it. Nobody knows how. Actually, you do know how, you're just a coward and you don't dare leave it behind. Leaving behind politics is going to be hard for anybody who tries to do it, because politics, sadly, is the number one rated show on cable TV, on network television, on the internet and everywhere else because it provides, as I've said a million times in a row, the reactions from social media to get the clicks. We keep it alive by participating in it. You and I keep it alive every time we participate in the political theater of the absurd. Now, there's a lot of people who are monetized to benefit from this, and you know who they are, but the only way to restore the American way of life is to reject politics at this time, especially if you are on the right, you must dive into the culture. You must follow me into the culture. And if you're not going to follow me into the culture and you think the culture is simply putting the latest slogan on a coffee cup and selling it to your fans?

You're part of the problem that plagues conservative minded voters. I hate to say it, but some of my favorite people are part of the problem, and the reason is they've monetized themselves into needing to operate this way. The politics of 2016-2022 has gotten us what on the right? What has it gotten us? Nothing. Zero, zip, nada. No culture, no influence, but lots of reactions. Lots of "Fuck Joe Biden" disguised as Let's Go Brandon on T-shirts and coffee cups have been sold. I mean, do you really think that this is a movement that's going to make any kind of headway other than enriching the people who are already on the stage participating in the market of reactions? Hell no. Your country is long gone if you keep tuned into this. I'm a life long registered Republican, and I would absolutely play this game with the Republicans if it was a fair fight. But it's not a fair fight. The game is rigged and the people who are on the other side of it are about to enjoy a two year taste of an increase in power. They're going to increase political theatre and that is going to increase all the divisions unless you boldly go where no modern conservative man has dared to go and that is away from politics and into the culture only. And there's nothing more terrifying than participating in the culture as a creator because you will be judged for your work. Politics is judgment free. It creates all kinds of rage, which means you've got people engaged, which means they're following and clicking and participating in your bullshit. But it's of no value whatsoever to the struggling common American family that is just looking for peace of mind and a peaceful existence and stories that edify their life choices as well. So the gaslighting happens because the culture is actually something that most of these paid professional Pundicrats do not possess the skills, the courage or the self control to not seek instant gratification. They lack these qualities that enable people to create culture, and that's why they only create chaos. One of my friends is a very successful hedge fund manager. And he had a political conversion during the Obama presidency that drew him into support of Republican policies for the first time. He got so into it that he decided to invest some of his money and start up a new right leaning media operation. This gentleman has a lot of wealth. He has enough wealth to really compete with a major network. And so he checks into a hotel in Washington, D.C. after putting out notice that he was going to start something new, and the resumes came flying in from every single person working in right wing media. He was confused by it because he thought people who were running successful operations already wouldn't be so eager to jump ship and join something new. And I said to him, this is what Conservatism Incorporated means. Conservatism Inc. is a monetized, reactionary, non lethal political entity. It has zero bite, zero influence, zero power. Instead, the folks on the right who are elected officials kind of move around the chessboard, never really increasing their power, but faithfully playing their part, while never reaching back into the arts. This lack of self-awareness edifies the left's culture at all times. It's a complete con against conservative voters. Conservatism Inc. is a disappointment to know that it exists, and it's really disappointing to understand that it's the main reason why the business of politics is so divisive. Division by storytelling is the low hanging fruit and its usefulness in the narrative is of critical importance to the system because the system cannot maintain its grip on power unless it distracts half the citizens and then agitates half of that half into being pure reactionaries. It sets up a situation for perpetual loss. Prove me wrong, where have we won? Where have we won in the culture? Clint Eastwood puts out the well done patriotic movie American Sniper and it makes $500 million at the box office and it's a preview of the system the way it should exist. But what did we gain from that? What did we gain as voters far from power? We didn't get more movies like Clint Eastwood's movie. We got less. We didn't get more patriotic embracing of Americas heroes. We got less. There's a reason for this. We're all conned by this dynamic that says if you're very, very, very political, you're virtuous and you're telling the truth and you're fighting the man and you're going to overcome the system by constantly holding your ground. That's wrong. You're going to overcome the system by subverting it, by becoming a sub pop culturist, by operating with indifference to the established sides, but with care and concern for your local community, your local experience, your fellow Americans. The system must be ignored so that its power cannot be increased. The more you pay attention to it, the more you become the spoon that feeds poison to your fellow Americans.

HOW TO KILL THE IP COLOSSUS

The book you are holding and the podcast it is a reiteration of, are both meant to cheerlead and encourage a brand new sub pop culture from the ground up. And the reason we have to do this is because the corporate pop culture that we all live with is poison, and we know it and we're not going to beat it by going mano a mano and building giant movie studios or funding more think tanks. We're only going to beat the system by coming from the ground up. It's our only choice, and that's why I'm doing this. Why confront when you can infiltrate and subvert?

The media colossus, from the television business to the movie business, really operates on one form of fuel and that is intellectual property. The studios acquire intellectual property and turn it into new intellectual property that they then license out. Edward Jay Epstein wrote some wonderful books about how the Hollywood economy works and what stuck out to me in the previous book of his that I read, called *Hollywood Economics* is that if a movie studio didn't have the ability to license out its IP to ancillary markets like airplanes, cable television, etc.— a studio would go bankrupt within weeks. That's how important that income is to the system and it's all possible because entertainment companies tie up the rights forever to intellectual property. One of the ways that they guarantee that there is no competition in the IP market is by setting all kinds of IP traps in place to attract you like a moth to a flame with your intellectual property so that you'll give it to the system for practically nothing. That's one of the reasons why I personally started to write novels that I could publish by myself as opposed to screenplays. Because why would you sign over your intellectual property rights to people that have the power to put it in a locker and throw away the key and nobody ever sees what you created? There's no long term value to that at all. Maybe you're lucky and your movie gets green-lit, it gets made, but then you're just put in a box and encouraged to write that same movie over and over again or whatever it is that you do, it must be repeated because the system is unable to feel—it can only sense "what works" based upon data that is colder than ice.

Intellectual property is what the closed system re-volves around. So we have to turn off the magnet. We have to turn off this river of flowing ideas that go exclu-sively to left run institutions. They like to set up film festivals but it's not really a place where what you think is going to happen, happens. It's a place to waste your time and take your intellectual property, expose it to the world—oops—it didn't get picked up by any distribu-tors. Now what? You're just floating off in a sea of noth-ingness. I've known so many filmmakers who've gotten into Sundance as the final act of their career. Sometimes you get an award or you make a deal, but even then it really never ever adds up to any kind of long term career because again, they're just acquiring that intellectual property and you have a timestamp on your head. There's only so much time that they're going to play ball with you, but they're going to keep that intellectual property forever and profit off it. So turn that tap off, and the movie business is over quickly.

Netflix has been the greatest threat to the studio system in my lifetime, and just like any studio, it must seek out and license material to produce into filmed entertainment, including optioning books by indie authors. This is where the business is heading—media conglomerates that have the money to produce and make content still have to go and find IP that can become that content, from somewhere. And right now, they're just going through all the same channels the system demands all go through, which is agents, managers, the Hollywood closed system, the intellectual property thieves and guardians of stolen treasure. But those walls are breaking down now and there's a really great story about a self published book called WOOL by Hugh Howey. He was an accountant, and his first book became a very successful indie science fiction novel—so successful that a publishing house made him a deal and picked it up for wider distribution. And then 21st Century Fox (now Disney) bought the underlying rights. Hugh didn't have an agent at the time. He was a guy just working out of nowhere, writing his intellectual property, owning it, and now he's reaping all the benefits of that independence. He didn't just write a spec screenplay and sell it. He's not a cog in the wheel. He goes off and he writes more books. He publishes more things. He's in control of his garden of ideas and any fruit that he grows, he can decide how to share it as opposed to giving the seeds to the people who don't like you and letting them hoard and only grow what they want, what serves their interests. And that's exactly what goes on in the intellectual property game; lots of diversions, lots of opportunities to expose IP, diminish its value, give it away for free, have it stolen from you. But if you take that creative process and you own it, and if you're a writer like myself and you begin to self-publish books, that's a great way to tell your story and be protected and have a copyright that is protected. If you are an indie filmmaker, why bother with film festivals anymore when the audience really doesn't care? It's an old shell of a business that doesn't really exist anymore, other than for the pleasure of the people that show up at the film festivals and go to the parties. And I even think that's getting boring for folks. We indie artists simply want to do business. We don't need a party sponsored by corporations. We want to do business. We want to have that independent folk filmmaker, a guy like Dan Lotz, who I see on Twitter and has all the right attitudes, the right approach and doesn't care about the rules that are established—just tell a story and get it to his audience. And that's what we all have to do times a million and we have to do that without ever looking at the mainstream corporate entertainment conglomerates as the final destination for our IP. The new relationship should be, *hey, if you guys want a piece of this you can license it from me. I'll sell it to you under my conditions.* We really can change the creator/studio/distributor relationship over time, but it's going to take, as I have said in my podcast episodes, about a 10 year period of indies not making a lot of money, but making a lot of cultural headway instead.

That's what we have to do. We have to make headway. We've got to turn off the tap. We've got to stop sending things to Hollywood in order to retain control over our intellectual property and therefore the culture. They can't write million dollar deals to everybody. We outnumber them. The creators that are independent and outside the system completely outnumber the compromised folks that are involved in the corporate storytelling that sells lifestyle masked as stories. So let's tell better stories. Let's keep our intellectual property all to ourselves, and let's play this game long and smart. Let's make them come to the table and ask us for a bite instead of just handing over the whole meal in hopes that it's liked. Your work will find an audience if you're persistent about sharing the work.

A lot of readers out there don't realize the battle for equality of thought and material opportunity within show business has been going on for a lot longer than many people know. I arrived in Hollywood in the late 1990s with the original screenplay Tigerland. It quickly became a feature film and launched the careers of Colin Farrell and Matthew Davis and I got thrust into the IP system as a result. I was invited to all the parties. I hung out with all the cool people. I did the meetings, I did the "dog and pony show"—but more than anything else, I did what writers do and paid very close attention and collected details that most ignore, and because of that I understand how the whole system works. So let me tell you now about all the failed attempts to organize conservatives into an artistic force that creates the culture. When I left Hollywood, it was around the year 2005 that I got out of there, and when I did, Andrew Breitbart had put out a book called Hollywood Interrupted. I picked it up and I read it. This book spoke to me like no book had ever spoken to me about the movie business, show business, the culture that I was living in. And I highly recommend you read it because it really does detail just the kind of debauchery that goes on—the kind of dark human nature that is cultivated and always on display among the rich and famous. People acting like pigs with money and sex and power just turned up to 100 and overflowing out of every tap. Show business is a nonstop orgy of worldliness. And Breitbart details that really well in the book, and it got me thinking about what the hell am I doing here? I don't operate this way naturally even though I tried to fit in. This is not what I'm here for. This isn't what I want to be a part of. This isn't why I chose to be a screenwriter, but it seems to be the final destination for all successful creators. So I pulled back in dismay and deeply depressed. Then Andrew put out a notice that he's starting a blog. He's going to go after Hollywood and needs contributors. I was one of the very first folks that signed up to contribute to Breitbart News when it was simple called "Big Hollywood." I wrote articles that reflected what I knew about the business, the double standard, the way that leftwing talent can do just about anything he wants and it'll be covered up, but if right wing talent gets caught one time doing one line of cocaine in one hotel room off the side of the road somewhere it becomes the scandal of a lifetime as if as if everybody is not human and makes mistakes, you know, just the left are human and worthy of your sympathy, but the right are subhuman, right? That's what we all know is their mantra now. So Andrew organized conservatives, and he organized them spectacularly with his website and he brought people back people from all over the nation. When I first got on the phone with him, he said, *"Come back, come back, we need to reset this business. We need to retake this town."* So I flew back to L.A. from NYC to attend many parties, many get togethers with thousands people. An organization had formed into a political minded group of artists that were defending storytelling and creativity and the ability to express yourself from a right wing conservative worldview, which isn't necessarily what the left tells you it is, but what we creators want to recreate more truthfully. Most people learn simple human truths through pop culture storytelling but audiences only get one side of the story when it comes to religious and conservative Americans. What Andrew started was meant to push back against it and looked like a really great setup. You've probably read about it. It is called *Friends of Abe*, because of Abraham Lincoln (the first Republican) and was inspired by *Friends of Dorothy*: the Dorothy Dandridge led club that many gay and closeted actors in the 1940s and 50s used to have secret meetings and feel comfortable being who they were away from the public. So Friends of Abe became the secret group of liberty loving friends centered around Abraham Lincoln's namesake for obvious reasons. But it never turned into what it was supposed to turn into. And the biggest party I went to was somewhere out at a private estate in Thousand Oaks, California. When Andrew was still alive, he said at this party, *"I want all the all the producers to stand up."* and all these producers stood up and, we're talking a star studded crowd with a lot of names and a lot of well-known faces and personalities. So all these producers stand up. Some of them have made huge feature films at studios. Some are independent guys with money. And then he says, *"now all the actor, writers and directors stand up."* And so I stand up because I'm a writer and all the actors and directors stand up too. And he said, *"now reach across the table and shake hands with each other and now go make art!"* — and wouldn't you know it, almost nothing lasting came of that moment. There's a few things that developed out of those relationships but nothing with a big impact on popular culture (where policy is normalized) itself. When I reached out to producers, it was the same brick wall that was always there. And I started to get the sense that this move to gather and urgently save the culture was just a disingenuous grift, not by Andrew, who was completely sincere. He was the guy who really broke through and told us that politics and narrative are one and the same, but there was no action. There was just division and opportunistic people seeing an opening into show business through political theatre. Over time it appears that bad folks pushed Andrew out of his own company. Things went south and it was just a weird situation that if you can get my drift seemed to no longer be centered on the central question of *"how are we going to change the culture?"* So that's what I center on with this book and my podcast, and that's why I'm never going to stop focusing you on understanding the nature of the system. I have never stopped being focused on the subject of culture. I'm here to create. You're here to create. And what we create becomes a reality, so we're not going to let ourselves fall into politics and becoming little political action committees for interests that don't benefit us. What we're going to do is create our own sub pop culture. If you want to be a part of our sub pop culture, God bless you. The easiest way to help is to seek and buy works from independent artists of all kinds. Or if you're an independent artist, release your stuff and try to make it work instead of making it big. Let's farmer's market our entertainment across the entire nation. We have to do it, if we don't do it, we're constantly caught in this honey trap, which tells you we're going to fix this one problem, but then always diverts you away from that one problem.

One thing you can count on is this grassroots effort will never divert from its goal, which is to inspire creators to create independently to distribute their work independently and to restore American independence in their stories. I'm not saying don't tell stories about this or that whatever story you want, but just keep the American culture alive within your story and that that really starts with not breaking people up into balkanized subcategories. If you want to tell a story about a person who's in a specific identity community these days, my advice to you would be to tell that story as is, without making a big splash about the individual group that person "identifies with" and in doing you you generate some unity by making the hero's struggle very specific and then it's universal and all will relate. And that's really the missing ingredient in our corporate stories. So I'll never stop pushing you in that direction, pushing listeners to support the truly indie arts.

My goals here are long term. I always play the long game and I've been patiently playing along with the right hand side of the aisle, trying to be a ground soldier who blogs and repeats all these things that are sold to us as a way to fight back and win the culture. But it's just disappointed me time after time and conservatives lose more and more cultural say in America every year. So let's stay focused on culture only. That's how we're going to flip the culture by organizing millions of folks tuned into this new marketplace, which is just a new mindset that prioritizes choosing indie American culture and art over corporate junk food entertainment and lifestyle.

NEVER BRING A
KNIFE TO A PEN
FIGHT

S tories paint pictures and pictures get hung on the
wall — when you surround yourself with enough
paintings that tell the same story you have the
culture. And that's why we have to change it. And that's
why I will never stop reiterating the point of this book,
which is to inspire you to change the culture with me, to
join me down the twisty path, to fight this good fight.

One mistake that the right constantly makes is it attempts to show up the left, is it says *just give us a movie
studio, give us hundreds of millions of dollars, we will
make the entertainment that the American people love.*
And that's the whole fight. But it's not. I support that
mission but it's the finish line, not the seed of change.
There's folks that I know at different companies trying
to raise money, and I have tried to help a few of them,
but every time I go to somebody who could potentially
invest in a new media company, they list the hundreds of
outlets of entertainment options that their family has
and ask why would we build another one? And the answer they're giving me led to the realization that what
I'm doing here at sub pop culture is the only true way
forward. That's why I'm taking this path. That's why
I'm trying to lead you down it because it is just about
organizing a community. There's a pretty famous com-

munity organizer who went on to become president, because when you organize a community you have the people. Now, in this case, I want to be the conduit which brings you into the right focus so that you can do the work of becoming the community, but right now, most of the work that people on the right are doing is wasting their time spotting hypocrisy everywhere. It has been monetized and the diversion is never going to go away. You will always have hypocrisy everywhere you look. This is one of the ways you can identify who is a helpful personality leading you to a better tomorrow or who is a charlatan or a grifter or somebody who is tasked with preoccupying the dummies for the benefit of the system. Any time you follow somebody on social media or watch them on television and they bring focus to a story and its conclusion is always just to point out the hypocrisy that has happened. Well, you just got conned for the millionth time. And you're smarter than that, you know better. You know it's the same hypocrisy over and over again and that nothing ever improves. And you should be wise enough by now to sense that it is a distraction so that you won't really fight and so that you won't really get organized so that you won't really develop a better mindset to win the game. You'll always be too busy putting out little fires or following the laser pointer and finding hypocrisy. And you're too busy posting on social media about it and you're too busy thinking about it and obsessing about it and stressing about it. But when are you going to focus long enough to do something about it? Because believe it or not, the most important, impactful thing you can do about hypocrisy is to stop pointing it out. By pointing it out, they have all of your attention. And by having all your attention, they make you useless against the system. So let's empower ourselves. Let's empower each other. Let's remind everybody on a daily basis and reiterate that there is no truth in the media. And so why bother even getting drawn into their bullshit game of spot the hypocrisy? We will have a big impact if enough people turn away because they'll have to find another jack in the box with better music that soothes and distracts you so that you'll be caught off guard once again. And those who are wise to this trick and speak out are cancelled publicly and then made into an example.

The 1959 television movie The Velvet Alley, written by Rod Serling tells you everything you need to know about cancel culture, whether it's Gina Carano or a newscaster or somebody who is a lower level media personality. It doesn't matter who you are. The equation is always the same. The fame, the glamor, the limelight, the money, is increased steadily, regularly, until it is your lifestyle. And then the system decides to turn on everyone at some point and use that lifestyle against them so that they can be forced to be an agent of the narrative that the system uses to maintain its spell over the American people. It is never a narrative that the people want. The people want entertainment and unity. The system wants perfect consumers who obey corporatized cultural leaders and embrace stories that reflect the life and the world and the values they want to sell you. The system wants stories that project falsehoods and aggravations and points of anger and touch-off moments to start new social movements and keep dividing the public by factors of one hundred. Over and over again. It is their business model and we cannot change it overnight.

If you were to pursue a career in show business and follow the traditional path straight to Hollywood, finding an agent and a manager, landing work, paying union fees, union dues, you might have a great career for a long time. Or you might have a short lived career, but one thing is certain—you'll be canceled eventually. Every celebrity is canceled as part of the system's self cleansing of overpriced talent deals. That's why cancel culture is here to stay. It's not new, it's just now well known. Talent has a shelf life. The great character actors are the greatest actors no matter what and they enjoy the best careers. The Martin Balsams of the world, the Nick Searcys—these are the true actors who can go on stage or on the screen and serve the craft to entertain an audience, but the difference is people who seek to become celebrities first and foremost in our hyper real world. And that's what most folks are aiming for. They're aiming to be celebrities. That's their craft. They're not aiming to be great actors. The people who succeed and become celebrities are then treated like a small company. The folks that represent celebs are invested to get percentages of their income and everything that they make. They are essentially shareholders in a small startup business, a small, high-risk startup business called Joe Actor and Joe Actor has the potential to make a tremendous amount of money very fast in a fast moving culture. Joe Actor has the right looks and he's a handsome small town rube who doesn't have the right team, so a team is built around him. That team includes an agent for doing the deals, a manager for doing the schmoozing and doing the deals, a publicist for keeping Joe Actor in the news, a stylist to keep Joe Actor looking good and a lawyer to make sure the deals are signed on the dotted line. On top of that, Uncle Sam takes a huge cut of everything Joe Actor makes as well. None of these services come free, of course. So Joe Actor's agent will take 10 %, his manager will take 15 %, his publicist will work for a fee or a percentage of what he makes and his lawyer will get 5% of everything. Joe Actor is a living advertisement of the Democrat Party's culture supremacy and a useful funnel to the big government folks who like to tax the shit out of everybody. So Joe Actor has a high tax rate, too. At the end of the day, Joe Actor is still a blue collar guy, and he needs that huge payday to maintain his appearance and career. He needs that regular money to maintain the dream lifestyle. At this point, the business has Joe Actor by the balls and Joe Actor will do anything that the business wants him to do. So I look at the talent reps as a whole, like corporate raiders that start small mini industries with these clients, and the industry is just that person's well-known name. Tom Cruise is a longstanding mini industry who has been profitable over and over again, but most people fall into the category of flash in the pan, quick money in and out, and those are the people that shouldn't even bother knocking on the door in the first place. In fact, nobody should knock on the door anymore because canceling is the ultimate destination for all who succeed. It's just a fact that canceling and cancel culture exists but now it's coming for indie artists who are monetized and built platforms for themselves where they are making a living essentially in show business without being inside the system. Those folks get coaxed into narrative traps and then are de-platformed the fastest. Right now monetized indie creators of all sizes represent the biggest threat to the organized manipulation and control of the national culture and narrative. And so cancel culture is the way to neutralize the threat but it's also dramatically used against famous artists inside the system—first by normalizing the practice with dramatic personal downfalls. The people who dole out grace in the form of fame and adoration, also orchestrate most falls from grace because that is how the system says intact.

The overwhelming narrative that we fight against comes from the top down and is directly opposed to the liberty giving narrative of We the People. And so if we can take more and more hearts and minds away from the divisive storytelling and focus it on a new grassroots movement like this country hasn't seen since the 1960s, we will have a shot at reversing the culture power away from corporations and back to the people. If we don't, then people will just be canceled as soon as they're successful because the system doesn't want competition. It wants consolidation instead. What I'm trying to grow here with your help is a very loud chorus of un-cancelable voices shouting and yelling to be heard, creating independent work and completely ignoring the system as if it doesn't exist. Because the system doesn't take you seriously at all so why should you take it seriously?

When you control the culture, you get to control both the lies and the truth, and the only thing the Left ever has for the Right is lies disguised as true. And so they feed us these lies and we take the rope, we grab it, we play the game of tug of war with the left, assuming it's a fair fight, assuming that everybody is in it for all the same reasons, but we only find out when it's too late, when we're all dangling off the other side of the bridge, the life leaving our movement's eyes as we're swaying in the wind. And we can only look at one another and say, *What just happened?* You know damn well what happened? We took the rope. We always do. And that's what we have to stop as well. Part of establishing our own sub pop culture means ignoring the other one and actively building a new one and ignoring the other one boils down to not taking the rope anymore. How do we get to this magical promised land that I'm preaching about where we control the rope? We must control the narrative and in doing that, we become the new symphonic reality. We already have the power. We're already there because one side of the media business doesn't want anything to do with half of this country, so half of this country should stop patronizing that side of the media business because there's enough creators and people of skill and know-how that can build the new culture I'm talking about. I'm here to inspire and get the conversation going in the right direction so we don't continually get hung up. We can't get loud unless we speak together. We can't speak together unless we all meet somewhere. So let's meet at the mindset of some pop culture. It's asking for nothing from you but a little bit of your attention to indie artists. That five minutes that you spent getting bent out of shape about hypocrisy? Spend five minutes on something that will upend the game as we know it. Check out the work that artists who love liberty are putting out. Check out the people I'm pointing you towards while checking out entirely of the corporate narrative because the narrative is poison to the American idea and wants to replace it with the technocrat nightmare.

TRAPPED IN THE
SECOND ACT

The culture works like a story. It has a beginning, a middle and an end. We find ourselves forever stuck in the middle. We're stuck in the middle because we don't control the culture. The beginning of a story starts with conflict. The conflict of our culture came in the 1960s when folks had organized the opposite of the way I'm organizing you. And they organized themselves to find acceptance, to find a new way to live their lifestyle, not hidden in shadows from the public.

That's the conflict. The course of action that followed was all kinds of people who shared their values that were in conflict with the popular culture of the time, which broadcast the established values. Determined to change the world, these people started to find homes in the companies and in the institutions that create culture, and work their way in from the mailroom, up from assistant, collecting connections from all different angles, they worked their way into the power positions at institutions that create and control the culture. Now the conflict of any story is what makes it interesting. You don't like watching a movie like Avatar because there's cool spaceships. You like watching Avatar because you don't know if Jake Sully is going to do the right thing and save the the the aliens from their oppressors, or if he's going to side with the humans, which is his own race. And that's the conflict. What I'm trying to tell you is conflict is always money. Conflict is drama. Conflict is what we're all stuck in because we just don't control this entire story. We're subjugated by a narrative that is projected onto us.

God knows people on the right hand side of the aisle or the reasonable side of the left (because there is one) have lost the battle over and over and over again to control the narrative. And because we're facing an enemy that is so powerful the conflict never goes away. The profiting and the rewards of that story being ongoing for most of our adult lives can't be brought to a conclusion until we have a true third act beginning, which is right now where everybody has the big realization of what has gone on in media and manipulation in American life. Everybody knows the truth now, and we're entering into the third act by some divine power, by some grace, by some miracle events that are going to happen. They're going to dramatically change the corporate left's hold on the culture, and we will get this third act to finalize itself to completion. And when the third act has reached its moment of truth, it's satisfying end, there should be an all new grassroots culture in this country that is ready to take its place. There should be a corporate culture as well, but it's going to be so well-defined that it's like choosing to go to a fast food drive through or staying home and having your mom's best meal that she always makes with all of her love. Those are going to be the choices in entertainment—junk food or stuff that's good for you.

Who distributes it? Who cares? That's not something that I think that us small people, us little indie artists, as folks trying to raise up a new culture, that's not something that I think is within our grasp right now. 10, 15 years from now, somebody reading this book is going to be on the receiving end of our hard work, and they're going to build those future organizations that are then dominating the culture in the same way that Facebook and Twitter and other companies are today. Hey, nothing lasts forever and there is nothing new under the Sun. Life is a story. Culture is a story fight, and we got to get ourselves out of this damn second act because it's killing all of us.

The reason the previous generation that controlled and operated Hollywood/American culture lost that culture battle, boils down to something unbelievably obvious, but at the same time, so hard for all of us to see. The conflicts and 2nd act material of the modern left are all conflicts that tie back to some form of personal identity or pleasure. The conflicts that the great storytellers focus on are not simply the boulder chasing Indiana Jones or something simplistic and over the top like that—they're the inner conversations that go on inside the heart and mind of a human being faced with making a good choice or a bad choice. But we're still stuck in the (corporate) second act and because the second act is the most profitable place for the media corporations who are keeping us here, there's a heaping of entertainment to encourage more and more diabolical behavior among the public, because it's like pouring gasoline on the second act only.

The conflict is well-established and never going away because these folks don't want it to go away, but that gasoline is going to get poured on that second act over and over again, and it's going to come at us in seemingly innocent ways. People love seeing the uncivil on display because the left has married flaunting and being an asshole to pleasure and power. And so when a character like Cruella shows up and burns her white dress off and it flames up and becomes red and she's all sassy, that's how they want you to be on the inside as well. Monkey see, monkey do—clearly. Very few people are really like that but we're existing in this separated cage match thunderdome called social media, and that's exactly how we treat each other. No longer human and instead we treat each other as these targets of our aggression in the perpetual second act. Because that's how we've been led by the corporate culture, but we can't stay here. It's not survivable by anyone. All it can do is tire you out, waste your time and then chew up and spit out the next group of people who come along thinking that, *"hey, now we've got a president who's going to change things."* None of that is going to change. It has to start with us. Entirely. That's our only way out, becoming like weeds that grow up around the legs of these power hungry folks and slow them down because we're getting trampled. So let's push ourselves to that third act by just walking out of the never-ending second act. Don't be players in the dark plot anymore.

I'm not saying that you change anything by just simply walking away. You have to do something positive in its place. This is not a time for choosing. This is a time for creating and restoring American culture. The people who come after a generation of independent pro-liberty creators will have the the ability to make a choice because they will be at the first act of a new story. The third act will have ended and people will find themselves in a world clearly defined because of transparency of how the system operates. Everybody in the government claims to want transparency. Transparency is not just seeing everything laid out on a table, through the window, but having a good understanding and having a clear definition of what precisely is going on with those things and how they work together. The folks who want to make a studio and produce movies for your family have no social conflict. That's why they don't get invited into the main stage because the main stage is just interested in making money off of our conflicts. So let's make the conflicts us, the people, the free people, the people of this country who built all the institutions in the first place. Let's make us the conflict against corporatism in storytelling because corporate storytelling is a scam against unity. And until we stop it, it will always work to divide us against ourselves, to maintain the conflict, to keep the fight going so that we never as a group get to that third act where the action starts to fall and the tension starts to fade away, and that peace and normalcy returns to our life that everybody seeks and everybody wants. And when we finally reach that Promised Land, storytelling will return to being about decisions about what's right and wrong instead of wind at the back of people who are professional assholes dominating their fellow human beings and participating in a dick measuring contest to see who has the most stuff.

Rejecting glamor isn't necessarily what you think it is—rejecting glamor is rejecting the glamorization of bad behavior that becomes food and encouragement for those who already have a large portion of their human nature turned to a side that cares less about others and more about themselves. This characterization of the American cultivated by the media only makes the corporations stronger and divides us so we will fall faster.

Paradigm Shift

The paradigm shift is underway, and it is not a shift from left to right. It is not a shift from more government to less government. It is not a shift to more truth and less lies. It's a shift to knowing, without a doubt that the whole world of corporate storytelling is designed to manipulate, cultivate and extrapolate resources, ideas and brainpower from the American people. All of it wrapped up into one big, ugly, bland, boring, flavorless junk food snack when really what we can start to see if we don't get sucked in, if we ignore every temptation to fall for some fake story about our neighbors, is we can begin to see the beautiful mystery because the beautiful mystery is what truly calls you. The beautiful mystery is what calls every artist, including artists who don't even have a faith. Artists seek communion with the mystery when they write music, when they create stories, when they create art, there's something mysterious and unknowable that can only be understood by our feeble human minds when we sub create the creator Himself. And that's what SubPopCult is trying to do—organize, inspire, but also raise up a generation of more responsible creators. The responsibility you have when you shape culture is massive. But it's shaped by humans, and humans have a massive problem: we're all flawed. We can't keep building sandcastles and expect them to stand. We have to start building our culture on the foundational things that are true. But one of the problems we face specifically on the right is those who are well-educated in the truth but also have a part of themselves that wants to play in the artists mystery sandbox are influencers typically pointing just to the finish line. (*This is the truth. Here's where you need to be. This is what's good for you. This is what's good for society. Do it. Do it now. Flip a switch. Fix our problems. Game over. I'm done. Make me rich.*) But that's not how the system works. Everything is a journey. You weren't born an adult. You were born a child and through your childhood you had many trials and tribulations. Many difficult lessons. Your life is a story happening in real time. And in your story, there's been drama, suspense, anticipation, tension, resolution, multiple stories, multiple seasons. You've seen relatives meet the end of their story. You've been introduced to new relatives who just appeared in this world brand new, starting their own unique story. But we can't demand that everybody go straight to the finish line and collect $200 for passing Go. We have to take them around the board, and by take them I mean we have to enable a true journey around the game board of life.

One of my main reasons that I cannot stand Big Government is not why you might think. For some, it's "Government won't let me do X, Y or Z." And I tend to agree with the desire to be free to do most things, but the real danger to Liberty is that the more the state can legislate and prevent the individual from falling, the less the individual will cry out to God (the granter of all human rights) and ask for help when nothing else worked. Calling out in a moment of total desperation is how many strong faiths begin. I'm sure you've heard the saying the road to Hell is paved with good intentions. Well, it's true. We are actually very far down the road to

Hell right now, and we've paved our way here with decades of good intentions. I think in a previous time when people who had control of the culture institutions and who were a little bit more mature (not so beholden to their personal desires to be the richest, the most famous, the most powerful, the most whatever in all of history) there was a common ground understanding that man is free, he's free to make mistakes, and he's free to seek help in the form of prayer. In the form of asking for the Lord to intervene. That was a commonly held value and so the government didn't legislate every little thing it could. Because the people had a relationship with something much bigger than Government. And that relationship was clearly represented in the culture. Faith in God was blended beneath the surface in the work, in the stories. They all contained the hint of the beautiful mystery. The most beloved works contained the beautiful mystery, the things you still watch to this day. Like, for example, *It's A Wonderful Life*. The film is overflowing with nudges about the existence of the beautiful mystery, but the Government wants to become God and there's only one way to do that when you're the Government: that is to remove God from the popular culture among the people.

Chesterton (Gilbert Kieth Chesterton) if you don't know who I'm talking about, is known as the Apostle of Common Sense. Some of his statements and some of his observations from long ago resonate so loudly today because the journey that we're all on, no matter where we are in it, is one of the big giant human family lost in a sea of its own misunderstandings. And there's a very clear, straightforward way to undo those misunderstandings, but it's not simple and it's not so sexy. The government removes God to become the God. So only we can put God back. Many people who have a strong faith who know that everything I'm saying is true and want nothing more than to be able to turn on the television, watch a show with their family and not have some sort of social engineering agenda that empowers the Government over God present. Instead, they would love to have (and I think I speak for the majority of people in this country of all faiths) stories that tell the truth about human nature, but leave open the possibility that something outside of human nature can have a profound impact. And Government is not outside of nature. Government is a direct reflection of human imperfection that has been converted into public policy and law to correct those imperfections, which now tears the nation apart, separating families and friends on the most ridiculous and meaningless grounds because it's almost impossible to see and wonder about the Mystery under these conditions. This is precisely why I do not tolerate political pundits anymore, because their way of making money, their style of staying in business, whether they know it or not, is actively burying the Mystery so that instead all that surfaces is things that make you angry and then Government solutions to those things.

Because angry people click.

So where can the Mystery be found since it's been slowly removed from the popular culture that once celebrated it and is now replaced by the tyranny of Government certainty which buried it? I can tell you my story because my story is based on my personal experiences after a childhood of being raised in a Godless and faithless household. And I mean Godless, not in the sense that He didn't exist, but He wasn't a big factor in any part of my young life other than there's a God and so what? I was kind of left to be raised by the pop culture that surrounded me, which is why I feel that what I'm telling you is uniquely on-point, because not only was I raised by that culture of my youth, I also succeeded in breaking into the industry that creates the culture and was drawn in by the one consistent thing that's always been advertised to be found at end of the secular rainbow—gold in the form of fame.

Fame looks fun. Fame looks like a license to do whatever you like when you're a young blue collar kid. And this is why so many of the folks who become well-known celebrities come from families that are broken. When you're a blue collar kid and the adults that were in your life didn't necessarily do the right thing by you when it comes to forming a moral center to help you not get knocked over by the world, you really don't have anything other to aim for. So you do what all of the leaders of the culture have done before you and still do to this day, you try to fill up on worldly power and try to get more of everything to fill that void deep down that can only be filled by the infinite. So how do you connect back to the Mystery when we are buried so far from it and there's so much noise preventing it and it's not really embedded in our stories, in our culture, how do we do it? Well, for me, it reappeared in my life when I became a dad, looking at my daughter did the trick. It humbled me. It made my heart melt. It made me turn very small. I couldn't believe what I was seeing in the eyes of a small child that I was responsible for. And I respect this new individual life so much that I wanted to make sure I gave it the best chance to make it through this maze of a world we live in, which has poisoned our perceptions to get what it wants. I realized the need to raise a stable person so that she can actually make the world a better place. And so the Mystery to me started with her, but it just blossomed every single day because I spent a lot of time at the park or the zoo. I spent a lot of time with a small, innocent child. And one thing that nobody tells you about becoming a parent, a parent who is emotionally and mentally present with your child, is that it becomes your second childhood. Even though many of us, myself included, don't have the best memories of our own time as young people being formed and learning and all that we go through, you really do get a "do over" when you become a parent and you are tasked with righting the wrongs. You get to create a better situation for the young person and the most incredible thing, the Mystery itself, becomes clear again. You get to look at the world through your child's eyes, and when you do that, you're now back seeing the Mystery. The wind blowing through the trees is wind blowing through trees, and it's unbelievably beautiful. The ocean is an ocean, and it's mesmerizing and large, and its horizon offers infinite hope. Hope has its source in the Mystery and you can feel it again. You've never hoped for anything while knowing how it was going to come to be. "I hope this happens. I hope we get out of this situation." But you don't have any certainty about how. And then something unexpected happens, and it's a miracle. And its grace. And it's that outside force penetrating, manipulating for all the right reasons, the situation you're in so that it can be more free and draw you closer to the Mystery itself.

After a decade of spending every waking moment with a young person from birth to their 10th birthday, I had been refreshed. I had been renewed. My connection to the Mystery was reestablished. It drew me in closer and closer so that I never lose sight of what actual beauty really is because beauty is the only way to save the world. And that's when I decided it was time to start creating again. I had no interest in writing movies, no interest in being a part of Hollywood because it looked like the place was permanently positioned to be an antagonist to all the things that I discovered were the true sources of joy in life in this world. And so I said, how can I use my vocation that I learned (writing/storytelling) to help increase the potential that more people catch sight of the mystery just to wonder what it is? And so I began to write books instead of screenplays and in those books. I made a commitment. They're all going to have something in them that is a reflection of God's truth—a little bit of the Mystery. This is basically the same formula that J.R.R. Tolkien used, which is if you sub create but you're inspired by the Creator, you will have little bits of truth in your work that despite your audience, despite how they feel, no matter how they view the world, those little bits of truth are keys that fits and unlocks the heart. And they say, I LOVE Lord of the Rings, but they don't really know why. But they will later in life, because the journey, no matter who you are, no matter how hard your blinders are attached to your head, eventually they're coming off either painfully or beautifully. And when they do come off, you will see the Beautiful Mystery again. And that is what we need to restore in our storytelling, in our songwriting and in everything that we create.

Embed the Mystery in your work. It's an invitation to the person who is on the receiving end. You're not preaching to them. You're not telling them they must go to church on Sunday, and must get on their knees and pray. Leave that part up to God. What you're telling them is, look at this beautiful thing. It has a source. Go and seek it.

TEASING OUT
THE GAME

I'd like to draw your attention to a course of action that is necessary to breaking free from the tyranny of divisive storytelling. It's called teasing out the game. The dictionary definition of tease out is to obtain by disentangling or freeing with a pointed instrument. Essentially, it means to unravel something. So let's unravel the knots that are preventing a new culture by maintaining an untrue narrative that hopes you'll never realize that you, the freethinking, opinionated, dreaming, difficult, mind changing, wishy washy living individual is the only blunt instrument in existence that can unravel the game. The secrets are only kept secret by those who knowingly conceal how the game works for their own standing in the political narrative, but that ended a year ago when I started the SubPopCult podcast/grassroots movement and finally someone started to tell you the truth.

The first time I really honed in on the phrase teasing out the game was way back in the year 1998, when I discovered a book written by a successful tech entrepreneur about children and computers in the early days of computer technology. I love this book. It became the one book that I always wanted to make into a movie. Let me tell you a little bit about this project, why the author (whom I will just call Misha) is relevant and why the author's relationship to George Soros and Media Matters for America was something I learned about long before the general public. Misha penned a fascinating story about one of the very first computer classes taught in a high school in America. It is set at Horace Mann High School in the Bronx, and it was about a young kid whose parents are divorced and he has to live with his father, who puts them in this school that he really doesn't belong in. And he finds himself attracted to this computer class that had a computer the size of a refrigerator. It's called a PDP-11 mainframe. The computer mainframe was donated by Digital Equipment Corporation in New Jersey because one of their employees decided that there was a relationship between kids and computers that needed to happen and he wanted to be one of the first pioneers to teach them the inner workings of the systems that would run their future world.

Fascinating concept. Great story. But what I saw was my generation's American Graffiti. American Graffiti was about car culture pulling up at the drive thru, hanging out, getting burgers at the joint, dancing, driving around that classic American 1950s early 60s life. Misha's book was about the generation of children who were first given smart toys in the form of basic computers that they then could write programing language for and learn how to manipulate the real world around them and essentially get a one time peek inside the system itself before the generations that followed had it closed and sealed, reducing most users to monkeys with a clicker looking into a window box. You don't really understand what's going on behind the screen. How a system is present and runs on small basic instructions based on user input. Just like the culture when it's organic and coming up from the people.

When you engage with an author and are turning their book into a screenplay to be made into a movie, a relationship naturally comes of it because there was a quite a few lunches, get togethers, lots of phone calls, things that make it easier for the book author to trust the screenwriter, and also for the screenwriter to get a deeper understanding of the material he's trying to bring to life. So I got to know Misha pretty well and we never ever discussed politics until one fateful day—I was present for a phone call that Misha received, indicating that George Soros was committed to putting the money behind Media Matters for America. Misha and I were having lunch at a trendy restaurant on Prince Street in New York City when this call came in. We did the usual small talk and gab about the project, but then his cell phone rang and it was a call he was desperately waiting for. He answered the phone. I watched as he listened. His eyes lit up. His words were something like, "He's going to do it? That's so great!" He hung up the phone. And I realized much later that I just witnessed history because when he told me that day that he was involved with a project with a bunch of people who would regularly meet in the Hamptons and that they had just secured some financing and that now they were going to be in business to start weaving new political narrative, new political opposition to the evil, tyrannical Republican Party of President George W. Bush.

The man on the other end of the phone call that day was Mr. David Brock. That's the front row seat I had to the moment when it was a business plan implemented to make reality no longer reality. To make confusion and doubt and bitterness and anger the dish du jour for the American public. Media Matters for America did so much damage to unity in this country. They claim their target was Republican misinformation but if you've listened to my episodes, you understand the real historical story is that there has never really been Republican opposition to anything the left has done. It's always been a co-opted side party that enables the left's tyranny of division for corporate profit.

Misha moved to Washington, D.C., with a whole group of people that were working on these George Soros funded projects together and for the duration of the Obama presidency, they lived it up, created division, worked on a assisting a government that only wanted to get bigger and bigger and bigger. And here's the kicker after Obama was done Misha moved to Canada, where he still lives to this day, still a successful tech entrepreneur.

We don't understand how the system works, who built it, why it works the way it does and how to manipulate it. The people that do know how to manipulate the system are the ones who are responsible for most of the grief and anxiety that we have towards each other. It's all phony baloney. They run and hide after they do the damage. In the meddlers absence, waves keep coming in and drowns a few of us with it each time. The main point I want you to extract from this is how can we end this tyranny of bad ideas, how can we tease out the game enough so that it is in broad daylight for all to see? And then we can finally start to realize that it's not us, it's them. Teasing out the game requires you to be inconsistent in order to acquire knowledge about all sides. It requires you to be a blunt object, not like President Trump, who came out and really let them have it with his words. That's great. I loved it. It was funny. People who took it too seriously are are the same people that don't know their gender. But to be a blunt object means to not be this perfect little round peg that fits in the perfect little slot that was cut out for you. Be different. Be unpredictable. Be inconsistent. Change your mind a lot. Act weird. Do things online that aren't reflective of who you really are because a lot of your interactions are run by algorithm and the only way to defeat an algorithm that is looking to subvert you and pit you against other people or send you into places where your time can be wasted unlimited forever—the only way to get around that is to not have the algorithm know exactly who you are at all times. So when you repeat the slogans, when you take the meme of the day and you start to share it, what you're doing is you're raising your hand and you're saying 'I'm one of theirs" and the other side is doing the same thing. I am one of theirs, but the difference is the other side—they run the entire show. They have overflow. They have some people who are like us that just signal and do nothing, but they're so vast, so powerful that is just their overflow, but that's all of us. We have to turn that part of our brain off for a short period of time. Schadenfreude is enjoyable in a sarcastic society, but we've had enough sarcasm. We truly need to defeat this evil vibe. To put it in protest language, this evil vibe must be overcome.

THE CAST OF
CHARACTERS

Have you been paying attention? Have you been following along? Have you finally seen with very clear eyes that the media operates with one voice and one purpose? That's to divide you and me to divide left from right to invert right from wrong to scramble your brain and keep you confused and easily mislead so that the game can go on, according to the plan that has always gone on. Divert the right wing base, inflate the left wing base, but at all times, it's the same people doing the same trick. We have to stop it, and I know you're seeing it and I know it's hard to ignore. As a matter of fact I know it's impossible to ignore because many of you are easily conned into going after has beens like Geraldo Rivera. This dinosaur from the 80s and the 90s is a convenient guy to pop up and piss you off for a day or two. Same with Bill Maher. It's all about moving the story through the news cycle according to a time schedule that is not yours, but the media's. By wasting our time, they increase their power, but by confusing us, they make it impossible for us to take that power back where it rightfully belongs. With We the People.

Here is the point that Americans can unite around, and it is a point that is going to be easy for some to embrace, difficult for others. But right now, we really have one major force of division, and it is fueled by something called corporatism. Corporatism is the corporate way of living. The corporate way of being. The corporate way of doing. It is boring, bland and just completely devoid of heart. But the entire media, all the personalities, and the majority of the TV shows, movies, and lots of literature is all secretly bumping you towards embracing corporatism as the way of life. We're in a brand war that is ridiculous. You have Chinese consumers who lured the United States corporations over and, you know, with our losers (as Trump would say) in American government didn't have the foresight to see where this could go and allowed it to happen. And so all these brands have tasted the world's largest middle class. You've heard me say that before, while they've tasted it, they were drawn in from Hollywood to Coke to Volvo. It doesn't matter what the brand is on a global scale, it wanted to participate in taking money from the Chinese people who suddenly had something to spend. But really, all those brands and all that manufacturing and all that know how being brought to China was simply to completely unpack the way the businesses work so that China could move away from being a manufacturer of poorly made goods to being a brand empire of intellectual property. And so we get attacked by Coke or Pepsi or Major League Baseball or whoever it is that decides not to side with the American people simply because of contracts, relationships, moneymaking potential they have in China. But the rug was pulled out from under many of these people, particularly Hollywood, who no longer has a locked in audience in China that wants to see its movies next will be the abandonment of of Coke. After that will be the abandonment of whatever next brand we think is the coolest thing Americans ever created. The Chinese will create a new version of it, their own version of it. And those 1.4 billion Chinese consumers will make those brands global leaders. Those brands will be tied to brand based storytelling. Our entire system. Everything we do as Americans has been stolen by China. China couldn't do it on their own.

China can remain communist and have a a grip on their people, on freedom and thought using a social credit system. All these ridiculous strings that come attached with being a Chinese citizen. But our brands and the stories that made them compelling were all tied to our story of freedom and liberty. That only started to change when those brands got brought to heel by a communist government. So when you are quick to defend a brand from the United States or attack one because it disappointed you in the way that it didn't stand up for what you believe in, that's not a fight you're going to win. Those brands are listening to only money, and they need money to survive. Everything is top heavy in America. Hollywood is top heavy. All of our corporations are top heavy. The only thing that's not top heavy and is free is us people. We are independent and able to create with our own hands, with our own hearts, with our own eyes, we can use our tools, we can see what our fellow citizens need and we can make it new. We're never going to defeat 1.4 billion people with purchasing power. The Laverne and Shirley world is over. There's no schlemiel schlimazel, there's just Communist Party talking points that must be reiterated and repeated to survive in a closed down society. This is why the folks in our government are also incredibly dangerous right now. They would love to tie this country up the same way China tied up its country. They would love to have the people addicted to brands and addicted to pleasure. Addicted to buying endless, pointless things so that the power could remain in the hands of a few. That Communist power structure that is a little bit Capitalist, but a whole bunch Communist and completely anti-human anti-freedom anti liberty is like a shining red ruby that some folks in our country see as the ultimate way to reach the desired future of total power consolidation. We have to show them differently. The future is not going to be automated and robotic. Maybe some of the future systems, maybe we send robots out into space, but there is no future where humanity is completely wiped out and we just become consumers. That is as close as you can get to the matrix as possible. Think about it. You're in a cocoon of products. You're surrounded by misinformation, but you're not really breathing air. You're not really living life. You're not really touching the mystery and seeing things that are moving you in a way that makes you consider the big questions. Instead, it's brand warfare, politics, identity politics, false information to make you panic for one week, replaced by more false information to make you panic the next week. Breaking out of this bubble, removing the mask, taking the bitter pill must be done on a daily basis until the playing board is reset. Use this book as your daily reminder. You have to wake up every day and say to yourself "what I see on the television and what I read on the internet is mostly false. But what I see in my fellow Americans eyes that I encounter at the grocery store on the way to work at the office, that's the truth." Because those interactions are true. The false interactions are vaporware that happen in the vapor space of online agitation. Don't fall for it. Instead, we have to really get creative. Start creating, create, create, create. If you spend eight hours creating something, even if it's never going to see the light of day, but you just hone your skills in some way, maybe it's woodworking, maybe you roast coffee, maybe you're a gardener, maybe you know how to build robotics or you're a computer programmer. Whatever it is, you have to reposition your mind into thinking that you're rebuilding America. Because guess what—you are. We have to. The writing is on the wall. The corporations hate us. The politicians want that power consolidated, and we have to show them that we reject it by embracing each other against corporatism.

Understand this America, we used to be the country that decided the way the world goes because branded storytelling that has narrative built in sold a lifestyle. If you want to live in the lifestyle of Communism, Fascism and all the isms that are bad for your freedom and bad for your heart and bad for the way of life and your entire existence, then do nothing but complain. And if you want to fix this thing, then you have to completely ignore the noise and start going about your business is if America was just founded and we are going to relaunch our way of life through all new products, all new stories, all new personalities out with the old and in with the new. Because by bringing in the new, we will restore the past because only the old are corrupt right now. Only people tied into a system that paid its biggest dividends by selling out America is selling out the American people and the American way. We don't have to accept this. As a matter of fact, I already have rejected it in my own life and I try to live by example. Buy American means, not just look for a brand that's made in the USA, but buy local American. This is going to be harder for people who live in some of the cities. But for all of us out in rural America, there is somebody local who will make just about anything and probably does. Let's go and restore all the mom and pop businesses. Let's not try to restore them to their previous iteration, which was attacked and robbed by globalists. Let's restore them to something more locally focused so that the American marketplace is as diverse as its people. And in those new brands and in those restored small towns and in those communities that reflect the craftsmanship, the know how to love the values of whatever community you're visiting. The regional business, whatever it is, that tapestry of different marketplaces that you can get in a car and drive to, that should be how we define diversity. Diversity isn't forcing to have five colored people, five asian people, five white people so that you have an equal amount of races. Diversity should be that when I go to a town in America, there's a barbecue place. It's the local place. The guy makes his own sauce. He's the hero. That's the brand everyone buys. Yeah, you can go to the grocery store and buy some conglomerate's brand or, you know, some international thing. But go buy that local guys sauce. Get your furniture made by the local guy who does it with his family and has done it for and has done it for 100 years. That diversity will naturally bring us all together because we'll appreciate each other's creations and each other's work. If you live on the Northeast, you know you can get in a car in Virginia and you can go state by state all the way up to Maine. And there's regional differences that are apparent and there's local brands and they're wonderful. And some of them have become national brands that are still American. But if you get in a car in California at the bottom of the state and you drive to the top, it's one note the whole way you'll pass a few meth sections, you'll pass a few, you know, really down downtrodden areas too, but this culture is just one note from top to bottom. California has always been the provider of entertainment and and our culture, and there was a saying that says, *when it's nine a.m. in New York, it's 1950 in California*. But really, the saying is now *how California goes is how the nation goes*, but California is no longer really representing our nation and its diversity, and instead is trying to force us all into its one note bland conformity. Reject this one note, bland culture that California is really trying to put on the rest of us and embrace the true diversity of the creations of our people.

United We Stand against corporatism. United, We Stand against the state, telling every American how they should think, feel and what they should believe. United

We Stand against selling our nation out to foreign lands via our brands and the things that we all made a success here in this country. United We Stand means being united against the forces that seek to divide us. No matter where or who they are.

ALAS, THEY'VE COME FOR DR. SEUSS

Alas, they've come for Dr. Seuss. They wish to hang him with a noose. They claim his tales were racist bent. They judged him fast, missed what he meant. But if we look inside his tales, you'll find the balance of the scales. Remember when Horton heard a who? And we heard the wisdom of the Lorax, too? The lesson behind Green Eggs and ham that changed the mind of I am. Remember, too, the rotten Grinch who once would never give even an inch. He taught us lessons one and all boys and girls big and small. So if you've judged his works as poor, you should reread them. I implore the man we know as Dr. Seuss turned our imaginations loose. His impact was beyond compare. He told us it was good to care, to accept the red, the blue, the green and on each other. We can lean. So if you still don't give an inch, your heart has hardened like The Grinch released The Grudge, The Hate, the rule and embrace the hope of Cindy Lou. We love Dr. Seuss. (Author Unknown)

I didn't write that. And the person who shared it on their Facebook page didn't write it and made it a point of stating "I don't know who wrote this, but it sounds like everyone needs to read it and share it. So please do." What makes this individual interesting is it's an individual who I know is a total left wing Democrat. Why that's interesting is Dr. Seuss was never canceled. As a matter of fact, this whole canceling of Dr. Seuss is just the third act in the weekly string along to keep any of us from ever building a new culture. So let's break it down, and let's see how this piece of the puzzle fits in the master plan to keep the new culture from ever appearing so that we are all beholden to the corporate culture that rules everything. In a little under one week since news broke that six of Dr. Seuss's books were no longer going to be published, the amount of content created to edify the idea that Dr. Seuss was canceled (which is false) is enough to keep social media lit up sharing, re-sharing and reinventing the same punchline based entirely on a lie. So who does this lie benefit the most? You're not going to believe it, but both sides of the fight now. I know that the reason the right doesn't really have a culture is our culture is completely political driven, and it's all about punditry, and it's all about making stars out of people who are political actors and not entertainers and artists who create and reflect culture. The corporate left owns the culture exclusively. They jump right into it, define it and demand that its reflected back to them in policy, and they get their way every single time. Diversions and distractions have to be kept alive because there's a vested interest in powerful people on both sides in keeping them alive. All I'm trying to do here with your help is get us all to understand what and who we're really up against so we don't fight against fake targets. And that brings me to the Dr. Seuss moment. This distraction serves both sides perfectly. The side that is in the mental gulag—the right where artists can never escape and they can never break out—are the first to be highly irritated that anyone would cancel any work whatsoever. So it increases the rage, it increases the ability to create memes and create little pithy things that people get to share among one another and feel like "Gotcha!" we just scored a point on you, sucker!

Donald Trump killed the terrorists. Joe Biden killed Dr. Seuss. Well, it's bullshit, and you have to accept that it's bullshit. Dr. Seuss's family is responsible for his books no longer being published (the six titles that they pulled back.) Yes, there were left wing think tanks that studied those titles, and yes, there was pressure put on them. But this move by Seuss's family is all a reaction to the culture itself. I really like to look at it as props, essentially, and what we have is weeds growing everywhere, and those weeds force you to have to deal with them. So because we don't grow, because we don't build, because we just react, we get to sit back and react to everything? What we now know is the truth, is that one side is running the table with changing the rules about the way life goes in America. And the other side is constantly caught in this honey trap of punditry politics that never leads to any cultural change that improves the quality of life for people on a day to day basis.

So how does the Dr. Seuss thing work for the left? Perfectly, because the folks who are in charge are above even coming down to this level of worrying about what's true or what's false. What they really do is they operate at the level of what's working to keep everybody scrambled and disrupted. And this works great. I joked on my Twitter account that there's probably somebody getting ready to attack Ritz crackers, but you know something, everything is going to get attacked that can be comically made to have you fight it and defend it with your life. All this is telling, which I've been saying week after week on my podcast. So who's the new Dr. Seuss? That's what I want to find. Dr. Seuss put truth in his storytelling and in his books for children, but he doesn't have the patent on those truths. He made those characters at that time and the art that told the story. He's had a very long run. Mickey Mouse goes into the public domain very soon. And the reason why Disney is reinventing Mickey Mouse over and over and over again is so that nobody can take that Mickey Mouse original public domain logo, make T-shirts and start printing money, selling them to Disney fans. So keeping things on lockdown is a way to guarantee that you get as much as you can out of the intellectual property over time. Dr. Seuss's brand is losing its value, and so it's an easy target. We need a new Dr. Seuss. That's really the bottom line here. Instead of getting entrapped by this and writing poems like the one that I shared or making memes or spending all their time scratching their head until there's a hole in it wondering how did this happen? Instead, we should just be asking where's the new Dr. Seuss types? Let's find them. Let's make them famous by buying all of their work. I don't know who he is. If you know who he is. Tell me.

I think it's of critical importance to operate the new way as opposed to the old way. I've been reviewing films on SubPopCult to try and promote indie artists. The first film was made for $3000 and it was incredible. *The Long Con* was directed by Dan Lotz and it blew my mind. It is remarkable what you can do with a small amount of money and a good understanding of story and a healthy imagination. It's exactly the approach I'm talking about in a scaled down entertainment business. We need people making new stuff. I have a friend who's working on his version of The Muppets, but it's not the Muppets. It's his own puppet show that he's been working on and developing for a long time. All of those things are needed so that cancel culture becomes a revenue killing culture of their own source material. They hurt themselves, so let them cancel Dr. Seuss. If you've got all the books, you've got all the books, but don't let them own and run with the next guy. Let's make that person independently successful. Let the left sink to the bottom of the ocean with two hundred and fifty million dollar movies that nobody wants to see because it's all about Balkanized Americans and all their weird little ways. They like stories about humans having sex with each other and finding gold in the dumbest places as a backdrop to preach that stupid social agenda instead of telling a story about people with a beginning, a middle and an end—with a good guy and a bad guy clearly defined. Let the system go off that cliff instead of what we're doing reacting to them. Right now they know we're the dumb ones, and we're eager to hang ourselves instead of doing the hard and thankless work of culture building. Let's not fall for the trick. Let the system hurt itself because that's what it does. They kill Harry Potter. That's revenue. That's intellectual property that is no longer of value. They kill Dr. Seuss. His library becomes less. Anything that they have their hands on that they're making money off of is the only stuff that we should be completely ignoring. Because that's the stuff that's going to be used against us anyway, so let's get a step ahead. This is a game and you can still buy those Dr. Seuss books. Those six books, they're not going to be reprinted this year. They're not taken out of circulation, even the New York Public Library still has it. Don't fall for it. Let's build and grow the new things that are not revenue streams for the system so that it can't put our intellectual property on like a sock puppet and attack us in a perverted upside down world theater show that we're all tuning into. Yeah, I'm repetitive. I reiterate the things that are important to stop people from tuning into the political theatre show. That's the whole point of the new reiteration.

If we can remember what it felt like to know that Donald Trump's election was stolen and that the reason why the whole world wasn't turned upside down because of it, is that culturally the folks on the left have a majority of citizens locked up in their own little pleasure palaces, always condoning what they want to do so that these folks feel like they got a win and some power over the system. So what's our problem? The rank and file voters on the right have the big issue in mind, which is the survival of everybody's liberty and freedom but we can't even address that problem, we won't get close to addressing that problem until we break out of this vicious cycle. Don't misunderstand me. I am a life long Republican and I believe the 2020 election was rigged, and I know there's not a damn thing we can do about it until we have a voice in the culture.

THE STORYTELLING FACTOR

It's time to take a serious look at how we got from January 6th to the midterm elections 2022 and the only thing that's happened is we've punched empty targets over and over again in the final bit of theater, the final bit of manufactured drama that drives everyone nuts and only lasted three or four days per "latest thing." Now if you've paid attention, if you spend your time on social media like I do and like many of the people who listen to podcasts do, there was an effort to make you think that there was a national shortage of fuel, and that just wasn't true. It started when a section of pipeline controlled by computer was hacked and was held for ransom. This happens all around the country where a system is held ransom. Police departments have this happen to them all the time. Institutions are always being attacked if they can afford to pay to unlock their own computer networks. That's why cybersecurity is an important part of what everybody does when they run an organization. And believe it or not, when the Biden administration said the pipeline hack was a private sector matter, meaning a private company was hacked and a private company has to deal with that, and it was not a national emergency—he was right. And by the way, the emergency laws that governors sign, just in case you didn't know, are tied to the releasing of assets or money that is needed to remedy the issue at hand. So there's fuel reserves. A governor signs an emergency declaration making that fuel accessible when it's usually set off to the side for just in case. Just in case happened and people lined up anyway, and they panicked and they thought it was the end of the world and they assumed it was going to spread to all 50 states because the right wing pundits were all about spreading fake news because it helped keep the pressure on the left but it's no pressure at all and these pundicrats don't realize that. Instead they have monetized your constant reactions to fake news. Reacting to fake news is not ending fake news, it's strengthening it. Everything that led from January to now has been fake and made up empty targets to waste your time and to prevent that moment we truly need called the right wing 1960s. It didn't show up because it was distracted away.

I have this horrible certainty of something that I presumed for a long time because it's undeniably true when you dwell on it. Everybody on the inside is essentially friends with one another. That's right. They're all on the same team. They project the fight so that we will adopt it and fight among ourselves always enabling them to consolidate power. Are you sick of the system and all of its characters consolidating power? I am. Are you sick of this game, which you thought was actually a back and forth where both sides gave and took? I am, because that's not what happens at all. Instead, we have a guy who we all fell in line behind, and he dangled in front of us the greatest policies that didn't stick. They were just temporary, just like Biden's temporary theater of the executive order. And we will line up behind this guy, and he tells us all about fake news. And we believe it because we know the news isn't telling us anything true about who we are. Everybody is a racist is no different than everybody is an anti-Semitic person is no different than whatever it is that people want to brand and accuse you of to put you in your place one way or another. So we're taught about fake news. We're taught about the narrative. We understand that the narrative is completely made up and it serves corporations. But no matter how much we understand that, we seem to forget that it's still fake even when it's telling you things that seem arbitrary and especially when it's telling you things that seem innocent. It's always fake when a Pundicrat (monetized right wing pundit) spend all of their journalistic time and energy directing your attention to insane human train wrecks they find. And you don't take any time out of your day to fact check that because it's too much to keep up with. Well, who's the one that really is part of fake news then? All of it is a mirage. There is no right wing with power. I'm sorry, we have to admit it now. There is no right because if there was, we wouldn't be handed these little booby prize fights and we wouldn't fight over them as if they had significant meaning. They have no meaning, there's nothing to them. It's empty. It's bullshit. How many of you still believe that Meghan Markle wants to run for president, which she won't. Do you see the pattern here? Every trivial thing that can inflame you is thrown down on you because you'll use your time to react.

Action and reaction: two words that make the world go around. One side of our political body is action, and the other side is reaction. Unless that reaction becomes a counterpunch, it's a waste of your time as a citizen. Start being a people of action despite the right being expertly disenfranchised by it's own people. And because of this, sometimes our actions have to be very, very small, very, very local. And that's the kind of action that's going to change things. We don't exist in a world where the mainstream media reiterates the things that get mass numbers of people out into the streets for our issues. We don't do that. We're not that crowd. We're a bunch of individual thinkers who know what's right and we cherish what's right. But we're constantly told someone's going to fix it. *"Just elect me, and I'm going to fix it. Just get behind me. Just stand with me."* It never gets fixed. Just stand with me, instantly turns into sit down and shut up the minute the person is elected. You have to take a wide angle view of political narrative over 40 to 50 years to start to see the pattern. Try to take a long long lens and look at the stories, look at how Nixon gave the left everything they wanted, and he was the first one canceled on the thinnest of lies. He did wrong things but it was nothing compared to what people get away with these days. That's not a whataboutism moment where I'm suggesting he got away with something bad then, and it's nothing compared to what they get away with here and now. That's not what I mean at all. What I mean is they established their game and they made it work for their long term goals. And by small degrees, they made it work until over time, slowly after an erosion of the good, the bad rose up and became total corruption from top to bottom. The fish stinks from the head down. And I'm sorry, a Donald Trump is not going to fix it. It's going to be only us who fix it. It has to be you and me. We the People.

Whomever we put in the White House as the next Republican, if they have some magic promise that they're going to flip a switch and the whole world is going to go back to the way it was and they use the same tactics that Trump used before, I hate to say it, but I have a feeling it will be just another con. It's another fake pretend insurgency. Because behind the scenes it's all the same people getting shuffled around in the back and remember they're all friends. So my dream is to turn the game around on them. My dream is to make it so that the people who are elected are scrambling to figure out why they can't get us under narrative control, why they can't figure out how to get us to pay attention to

them more. We have to ignore the show. That's how we
decide. That's how we slowly remove their power is we
ignore them completely. Go about your basic, basic
business. Get your groceries. Take care of your family.
Put on Netflix and watch whatever you want. You're
not going to change a damn thing by canceling Netflix
or boycotting Ben and Jerry's. But what you are going to
do is when you turn down the fire on that political nonsense, is you're going to start to see a little more clearly
what we all need to do as a community and as people to
get to the benefit of having the government represent us
again because it doesn't represent us anymore. Government represents corporations and corporations have
markets of people that they have established and the
people who live in these markets spend money on the
products the corporations have to sell. And they don't
want that closed loop to go away. They use con-
sumerism to Balkanize anyone and everyone. This works
extremely well to destabilize any potential unity among
the people.

One thing I've noticed about the business practice
of breaking apart the whole to increase profits became
clear to me when I started to see all the different varia-
tions of cannabis products. Hear me out on this example because it also applies to humans. Twenty five
years ago, weed was weed. You went out and you said to
the guy, *"Hey, you got a bag of weed?"* And he said,
"Here's your bag of weed." and then you would take it
home and you'd smoke it and you had weed. And that's
all it was. It was a little bag of a plant that people like to
smoke. Then CBD came along. CBD was created when
growers took one part of that plant that has one feature
and they isolated it and created a billion dollar industry
with one part of that plant. Now you can buy other
parts like CBD, CBG, CBC and many more. Entrepre-
neurs broke the plant down into a million different little
tiny businesses that all have their own audience and

profit off of something that as a whole didn't sell for as much money. Same with concentrates and vaporizers. All of these different ways, these delivery systems, they're just breaking apart the whole thing into multiple markets. That's exactly what they did to the American people but it is not what they can do to the Chinese people. It's different, but to the American people, yeah, we're all dual loyalists. You have people who are like, *"I'm an American, but actually I'm an LGBTQ American* or *I'm an African-American* or *I'm an Asian-American"*, or this other kind of American. Corporations have taken these brands of races and put on them characteristics that aren't real in some cases and some that are real. But the point is they desire to break these "race brands" up into different parts when the whole human being is who we truly are. We're all human beings, so they break all the human beings up into their most basic characterizations. The marketing business and the advertising business can turn the whole into all these different profitable parts by pitting them against one another based on lies and storytelling. And so that's why you now have these special months or days now that celebrates a product—its iPhone month, it's shoelace month, it's all getting you to celebrate something and buy more of it on that day. It's national Donut Day! Everyone runs out and gets donuts. These are just ways to just keep inflating the economy but they also train you to perceive an ever changing landscape of what you should care about and when. You need to get an iPhone every two years because if they built one that lasted forever, the economy wouldn't be so healthy. These large volume repeat purchases are truly what makes the economy hum.

So how do we get a humming economy with repeat purchases to work for us conservative and nuanced Americans? Because the way that it operates is by heavily encouraging a race to the top of a pile of gold where you can stake your claim, and that's never really been a problem because it always existed in America, far outside of the simple life lived by people who go about their business and live simply, which is the majority of people in this country and in this world. Life is a very dramatic temporary event on planet Earth that everybody understands in large numbers in the public. And so we go about our business very simply. But the reason why it worked before is because what we saw in our entertainment and in our art reflected back that simplicity and that simplicity was desired and beautiful when it was revered properly. When you make entertainment that celebrates the simplicity but doesn't lie about human nature, humor and the bizarre dramas of life, but is removed from extreme political polarization and instead tells stories about who we truly are, is when the simplicity will be honored, edified and allowed to take root again. We'll get to go about our business and the people who participate in the other part of the culture: the the inflation of things, the fame business, the media business, all that stuff—they can go ahead and that take that journey and pay the price for it and it won't conflict with all of us regular folks who are just going about our business simply. Where the media elite went too far and where they may have gone so far that there's no coming back, is they started to invade our basic American culture itself. They started to mock the things that we hold dear. The simple things like sitting home after a nice meal with my family and laughing about something that we have watched on the television together and then making dessert, having a little bedtime conversation, just hanging out with your family, talking about life, daydreaming, encouraging each other to do better on whatever it is we're doing. That's the golden life that really, truly is the happiest moments you'll ever have. But we got invaded by this cancer of an incessant need to completely redo the culture from the left. Why are they going to redo the culture? Why can't they just leave the culture alone? Well, there's so many different reasons we can talk about it for hours but basically what happened is they monetized the balkanization. That's right, they monetized the balkanization of American people specifically as a profitable distraction to allow them to serve a bigger audience, the Chinese audience, by giving us toys to play with in the form of identity politics and gender pronouns and pleasure as the height of human experience. The pleasure of pride for all the bad things about human nature is a cancer on society. The corporate culture mantra is to be proud of your greed. It's spike the football culture, spike it everywhere you can get one up on the other guy, everywhere you can humiliate your opposite. The media blew Americans up like a tire. But it's going to pop and deflate when we pop it ourselves and we deflate it and we ignore the dark nudge, only then we can fill it up again with unity and get this country rolling because we are really not opposed to each other in America like the media portrays. The media just wants us to be active participants in their business plan of divide, conquer, sell, sub-divide, conquer again and sell some more.

So what is the People's Business Plan? The People's Business Plan should be to reject division and a parallel economy. It's un-American. It's the most un-American thing there is. We went from the melting pot to no, you're not welcome here. And so we have to turn back into the melting pot. That's the only form where all different parts of the human being become one that I accept. All of our passions and all of our political differences can still exist, but there's one place where we can never let anyone disturb us and that is in the unifying view that liberty—the idea that man's personal liberty comes from God is possible because of the free will that God gave us. It's true love. We have to all agree that we're free and that the most important thing is to be

free. And we have to be on the lookout for anybody that
tweaks our system and infects our system with devices
that erode that understanding at first and then flips the
switch when nobody's looking. We're at the switch flip-
ping moment, but we actually can flip the biggest switch
of them all by getting back into the melting pot and pro-
claiming we are all Americans despite our different cultures that we come from. We all value liberty. Despite
the differences in our religious faiths, we all value the
ability to have that faith freely despite every difference
that we have. The one difference we have as a country is
we are the United States of America, a land of free
people whose main priority is preserving that freedom,
which allows them to truly experience life and all of its
mysteries.

ARE YOU PAYING
ATTENTION YET

How many times have you seen your favorite Pundicrats and the people you follow online, beat you over the heard with this line? This invitation is a worm on a hook to keep paying attention. Do you know what paying attention is? It's paying with your attention. Think about that. Time is money. Time is limited. You make deposits every day into the life of other people who are simply slinging bullshit to keep the public divided and engaged in a one-sided fight that spoofs us into believing otherwise. Think about this—what is the incentive for anybody who gets into punditry, which is the cheap, ugly man's way into fame? The cheap, ugly man's way into fame is incentivized by political issues that are divisive, work against unity and at all times have one goal in mind, which is you paying attention to them who create nothing, who build nothing, who don't enrich your life at a local level at all. Instead, they just want to waste your time cheering on their grift. Your time is yours and your time is better spent on you. You can come together with like minded folks and you can spend time together building a culture community instead of toxic political theatre.

I want to give a shout out to the folks who put together BasedCon. I just saw the birth of an interesting community of artists. I know some of the people in-volved and I know some of the folks online that I in-teract with and I'm looking forward to attending next year because it was a gathering of folks agreeing to use their time in a positive way in that crowd of creators and writers and storytellers there is likely a budding J.R.R. Tolkien or a young C.S. Lewis with the talent to become next culture voice, but these indie voices must be culti-vated, watered and cared for. And you must understand when something is worth your time versus when some-thing is a waste of your time. That's up to you to decide, but the proof is in the pudding because if you have been paying attention, you now realize that this is the big con of political division—the left owns the power and they also own the right. And the right is mainly a distraction so that the state can do what it wants and consolidate power. I'm going to repeat this in one way or another, in a new way every time I can, because every week, every day, every post by a Pundicrat is just a repetition of something that they know will trigger you into paying attention to the grift. That's why they check in—are you paying attention yet? That is a tactic to frighten you into believing there's a coming storm that you cannot avoid and that that storm is going to engulf you, your family, your country and everyone—when you know damn well it's not true.

Be reasonable. There are good people and bad peo-ple. This is common sense. Common sense is obliterated by political nonsense. When I first got on a bus many years ago in my small town and I decided to move to New York City to spend my time pursuing a career as an actor, as a writer, as somebody who participated in the creation of film and television entertainment, some-thing that I loved and something that I grew up on, it didn't take long for me to realize that many people, per-haps too many people, have answered this call and we're on this same journey. And it was only when I made it all the way to Hollywood and broke through those systematic hurdles that are in the way and I cleverly got through and pushed my material in front of the right people and got a movie made, when I realized there's something going on that is trying to incentivize people to waste their time in pursuit of fame, not the creation of good entertainment. You learn this pretty quickly because the culture in show business is exactly the same as the culture in politics: smash and grab, let me take what I can get before you can even get your shoes tied. But currently the game revolves around the individual making themselves the center of all controversy and attention. The old saying that Michael Jackson's father believed, which was, *it doesn't matter if it's good news or bad news, you just have to be in the news*, is fact. Think about the characters who maintain their presence in your peripheral vision, your front view and all around you by simply being characters that are always talked about good or bad. That is part of the trick of getting you to pay with your attention. And the same thing has happened in politics, in monetized punditry politics. I was on the ground floor of the launch of Breitbart.com. I knew Andrew Breitbart in real life. I went to all the parties. I've been a part of that movement, which was falsely sold to me as a way to fix the culture. But it was never going to really work for this goal, it was another con-job way to begin permanently dividing the culture and monetizing the powerless side's reactions and I totally reject that. I want no part of bitter unsolvable division. It is unAmerican, whereas disagreement and reasonable debate over solutions is American. That's why the *are you paying attention crowd* is constantly drawing you into unreasonable, combative arguments—so that you will never return to classic Americanism, which is missing from our lives.

Americanism exists in the middle. The middle is where all things melt into the melting pot and become

American. What's being whipped now is separating the ingredients into opposite corners so they never come together. So that the taste is always horrible, flat and unfulfilling. And it keeps you coming back wondering why everything tastes like garbage. So be prepared because this call that I'm making, this plea that I'm saying to you about coming to the middle and ignoring politics is going to be attacked by the Pundicrats and by the main stream media class who will try to prevent any unity between the midterms and the 2024 Presidential election. They must get everybody evenly divided into powerless camps that are just reactionaries to the storytellers that they follow. And the biggest attacks always happen when we get closer to an election and it happens year after year after year. The system expedites attacks on anybody who wants to exist in the reasonable middle where just about every single person lives in reality. Pundits create a winner take all scenario when that is actually the opposite of the American way for Americans who are born in the United States or who are lucky enough to have citizenship here and be transplants to our country. We can't let them take our treasure, which is our middle. They're eating us alive and we pay for it with our attention. I know that pulling away from politics entirely is impossible because politics has become the popular form of entertainment at this time in our lives. That's very unfortunate. But in order to work against it, we have to be more like the folks who got together at BasedCon and decided it was better to spend their time building than destroying and reacting. There is an important distinction between anything that you do that is political versus creative or for your own well-being. Everything you do political is a reaction. Maybe you write a blog post here or there, but your blog post is also a reaction. The folks who are becoming the cable news talking heads of the future are no different than the cable news talking heads of the past. I guess the one difference if I had to really point one out is that there's so many of them because the creator economy to them is creating more political nonsense. But the creator economy, in its reality, is creating culture and content and living your life as an American and being free and embracing your freedom, which means you can change your mind at any time about anything. That is the gift of freedom. You're not stuck. You don't have to be wedged into one corner or the other. You are free to float between realities and between platforms, and you can find things on both sides that you agree with and like. I am a conservative, but I am reasonable and if we had more reasonable conservatives rank and file, we'd have more conservatives. The extremes only remove power from one side, the right.

Let me end this chapter by reminding you of the all important tool that helps you escape political nonsense: become ideologically impure! Everybody on the left or the right who is a pundit personality that tries to inspire you to move into their monetized and ghettoized corner? Resist. That's the real resistance. Resist, resist, resist. Find your way to the middle where everybody likes to operate, or everybody needs to live so that we can restore order and peace to the American way of life.

IT COMES AND GOES
IN WAVES

There's a lot going on, but there's also not a lot going on. Isn't it kind of strange how the political narrative game comes in and out like waves of anger, waves of misinformation, but then goes away and there's like a calm cooling period? That fluctuation in aggravating news and then dialed down news is just the media schedule going according to its own plan. And to us, it feels like things are happening and then things are not happening. What is the purpose of the hot/cold broadcasting schedule? Is it to agitate and draw you deeper into a political battle at times and then let the foot off the gas just a little bit so everybody turns to their personal life, which needs their attention and starts dealing with their kids or something else? You fill your time with something non aggravating just long enough so that your memory gets a little bit foggy about what you were mad about just two weeks ago, and then the stage is set for the next flaming lie and the news narrative comes out and—boom—everybody is glued to the screen, getting agitated over something new and then reiterating bad ideas that were crafted somewhere well hidden from the audience and their purpose is to make sure that only the bad and divisive ideas are reiterated so it becomes the the new reality. I believe that trick is coming to an end. I think people are wise to it now. And one of the ways you can tell that trick is coming to an end is the pauses are longer now and the moments where we're agitated by the news (and I don't mean just the news, as in ABC, CBS, NBC) I mean that hidden world of news agitators, the people that I call Pundicrats on the right or assholes on the left, because they're all the same people, they're all doing the same thing. They're into this monetized, divisive culture that we live in, and they've all got little businesses running where they take advantage of the false outrage. They are all outrage peddlers.

I've been doing the SubPopCult podcast every week since the 2020 election to draw us into an understanding of how the outrage is turned up and down and up and down. What it does, and I think everybody knows now that I'm telling you the absolute truth, is it prevents only one group of people from organizing. And by preventing one group of people from organizing the game just goes on but it feels like the game is going to come to an end in a way that nobody understands because we've been told all the lies so many times we are confused. With social media there's this bounce back where, secretly, some of us can whisper out into the world opposite storylines and those things get into into people's brains just like the fake storylines. And they start the the individual asking questions. When those questions are asked and when people genuinely start to question everything, not just question the left or question the right, but once you start to really question every single thing that is told to you and you juxtapose it with corporate interests and the selling of products and the creation of markets, you realize that all storytelling is only serving that purpose alone! It has nothing to do with what you passionately believe in. They really get us with this trick all the time by making us passionately fight for things that are only tools to the corporate left, only tools to the technocrat right, to keep you outraged, to keep you clicking. But I want to get you outraged about something else. I want to get you outraged about the fact that you keep clicking. I want you to get pissed off at yourself for constantly being distracted by utter nonsense. I want you to go back and count all the years in the Trump administration that you reacted to and fought over the left's disingenuous fake theatrical attempts to distract us, which worked, and then figure out what you could have achieved in those four years instead of a litany of tweets, angry articles and essentially nothing to show for it other than empty pockets and no political power.

So let me take out my crystal ball, and let's take a look at how the next four years are going to go. Based on everything that we know about storytelling, narrative storytelling and the hot-button issues that never go away that are just recycled. One thing is for sure (you can you can take this to the bank) any time there is a Democrat president who has won the presidency, it doesn't matter how dubious it is, it doesn't matter what the deal is with the troops, with the stealing—just hear me out—there's a Democrat who's POTUS and there's a Democrat Congress. And there's a tie in the Senate. And any time that happens, what follows it, this is crazy, you're not even going to believe it, are ready for this? A Republican president, a Republican Congress and a Republican Senate? Go ahead. Go back. Go and look at all the exchanges of power in the history of our country. Post Civil War. That's it. As soon as one side gets everything, the other side comes right in to take it away. But something happened in modern history where the sides don't take anything away from each other. Instead they're putting on a show for us and pretending to take things away from each other because behind the scenes they are in total lockstep and growth of the government is their mission.

I believe Ted Cruz really believes what he says about constitutional law but I also know that human nature is typically much stronger than someone's projected values. One of the reasons why I avoid going for the Hollywood power that I had my fingers within inches of, is because of its all corrupting power, and I don't want that to happen to myself because the current system is set up to make you end up at that conclusion anyway. That's the unavoidable fate of anybody who goes for the brass ring. You end up getting it and your only way to benefit from it is to grip it tighter and tighter and tighter, and then as other people try to come for it, you beat them down with a stick. I guess this is what the left says is capitalism, but it's not. It's unchallanged greed, it's absolute human animal nature, and it's the human mind cleverly making the excuse that this is capitalism, and this is why they're basically admitting that human beings on the left have zero self-control whatsoever and it must be accepted and tolerated. We can't police ourselves. We can't help it. You put a candy dish in the middle of the room and I'm going to go and take that candy because I'm hooked on it because my raw human nature pulls me to it, no matter what. But that's not always true, because there are people who have the ability to keep themselves in check. It is the mark of a civilized, modern individual to be able to subdue their human nature to prevent the worst of themselves from coming out. And sometimes that is understanding that you can't get too close to the fire because you're weak to it and sometimes it's lying to yourself and saying I'm stronger than the fire itself so I can go and play in the sandbox, but it burns everybody. It really doesn't matter who you are, it's just the amount of time that it takes. And so while the great storylines of success are shared with us, we've all watched Bill Gates rise to the richest man in the world and be on the cover of magazines and become important—but all of that importance was projected onto him because of this business that he built and the things that he's done. And recently he was tossed out by the news cycle as last week's trash. And so the narrative behind the narrative, which really controls the perceived realities of what a lot of us see and hear every day, used Bill Gates as a boogeyman the pundits framed him. He was going to poison you. He's got all the farms. He's going to do all these terrible things when it turns out, really, he's just a pervert dork who used his wealth and money to pay for strippers and meddle with vaccines. He's essentially a human being, just like anyone else but his mistakes are much bigger than yours and they effect you most in your imagination.

Human nature is present in us all. The higher up you go and the more power you get close to, the more extreme versions of it you're going to find concealed within everybody. The general public can wear it out on the streets. Look at the social media sites and all the young people on Instagram. They're practically taking off all their clothes and pulling their their legs open and saying, *come get it. This is my dance move. But come get it.* That's what's going on inside the hearts and minds of the Bill Gates of the world, too. It's just hidden by layers of wealth and corporate money walls that you can't see through. So our culture needs role models, and those role models need to be good role models. But instead, what we have is a culture that is watching people grab the brass ring, become the most important powerful person in the world to the media for a limited amount of time, and then the stage is set for the destruction of that character. It's the build up of man and the destruction of man. It's a systematic theatrical playing out of the truth of what happens in the world. You are not of this world and you not staying in this world. So the real currency, the real wealth that you have is your time. Your time is your money. So stop letting your time be robbed from you on these bad actors and instead use it towards truly building what we all say and know needs to be done: we have to rebuild our American institutions locally, and then we have to grow them into the future because the future is going to rely on the planting of new mustard seeds by people of faith and good will who stick to the plan, stay focused on the goal and don't waste their time getting caught up in the theater of distraction, but instead put one foot in front of the other day after day, slowly rebuilding, rippling out like a rock tossed into a pond so that we all intersect at a place of progress, not progressiveness, but progress, personal progress, community progress, progress in restoring the values to the way of life that we all simply need to live and live loudly for them to be restored.

HOOKED

Here we are entering into winter. Kids are back to school and like magic, we're all hooked on political narrative that devours all reasonable people. We're always hooked right in to the most dramatic part of the narrative—the second act—which never ends and never will end until we force its hand. And the reason it won't end is because it fuels the consolidation of power. I say that over and over again, because it must be constantly reiterated and internalized and you must accept it as fact. The more divided Americans become, the easier it is for the system to consolidate power among a few. There are so many storylines and overlapping parts of the narrative converging at this moment to make sure that each and every one of us has a healthy dose of outrage, disgust and anger at our fellow Americans. And the way that they pulled it off this season is by once again throwing a molotov cocktail in the form of the President Biden coming out and declaring half of the nation to be right wing extremists who are likely to commit acts of terror. But at the same time and in the same breath, ridiculing Americans who have not been vaccinated and declaring that he would sign an executive order forcing private companies that employ more than 100 people to have their employees vaccinated. Now this I noted in my mind when it happened, even though I had a reaction to it myself because it's actually the place that the government cannot go. It cannot dictate to the private sector how it treats its private citizens, it cannot overreach the elected governors that we have elected in our own states and tell them how to deal with the situation that doesn't come under the federal government's power. And so this was a moment of truth, and the true thing is because this podcast/book is about a narrative, the narrative, how to understand it, how to see what's happening is that the Republican Party is now starting to counter the story and change it to their favor. And the way they're doing it and how I know it's happening is because immediately after Biden's announcement, there was a cascade effect of the same talking points being reiterated across Republican governors, right wing personalities, media people who are connected to the right wing, independent, monetized punditry class. All of them together had a very similar script. We hire more than 100 people and we're not going to. We're not going to participate. We're not going to go through with this or honor your ridiculous request. Governors like McMaster in South Carolina were very dramatic in their wording. He said he would fight the Biden administration all the way to the gates of Hell. This is good. This is a good development for people who are seeking an alternative to a government that is out of control. Now, reiteration is a telltale sign of organization in this case, when the left has something or somebody that they want to attack. Have you ever noticed that the attack always begins, reiterated across multiple accounts? Some that are well known, some that are unknown. But it's always the word fuck. And then the person that they're going to go after next. I feel in many ways that it could be how things are coordinated. Lately, it's been fuck DeSantis. And then what follows that is an organized attack spread out among all the legions of people who reiterate that side. Now, conservatives have been lost in the woods. We've had very few things to reiterate that were not based on attacking empty, hollow targets. But now these Republican governors and their people in the media (who are only there to not have to get a real job), are all forced into reiterating something that is going to stick and is going to resonate with all of us. And so we should support it when that happens. And we should begin to understand how we can slide up to this narrative, participate in seeing it through so that it builds upon the truths that we all hold dear and spreads them to people who don't understand or see what's going on, that liberty is the most important thing to defend and that the government cannot continue to erode our personal liberty under the guise of trying to help us. So now that we have the seed of a new narrative that will work and will edify the things that we need to have established in our society to restore order peace in the American way, how can we, as artists and creators and filmmakers and storytellers and painters, how can we turn the culture in such a way that it marries up to this narrative? By doing so, we start to see the very first beginnings of the power that the Left has enjoyed for 40 years. We need an artistic community that is creating the mindset of independence, creating art that cause people to understand freedom and their liberty is dependent on the government being smaller. Now, that doesn't mean that everything has to be a politicized piece of work. It means you have to be clever and you have to tell stories with characters who face great cold opposition, careless giant systems that abuse their individual rights and treat them as data on a page. Not a person with a soul. There has to be musicians, not musicians and bands who write songs that hit the nail on the head, but songs that call out, celebrate and spread the message of liberty and freedom. The way it happened in the 60s was so successful that to this day, the left is still summoning all of their

1960s idols and songs. And it is a language that the culture speaks and the people understand. When the statue of Robert E. Lee came down the citizens were all celebrating the moment of "feeling" that they overcame some oppression by being serious adults, were chanting the chorus to the song *Na na hey, hey, kiss him goodbye* because the public speaks culture. The public does not speak policy. It understands policy through culture. And if you look at all the artwork and the creations of the left for the past 40 or 50 years, they have planted all the seeds that grew into the trees that now produce the bitter fruit. So we have to do a better job redoing the garden, redoing the plantation of ideas that we feed ourselves with. And please don't misunderstand me. I'm not suggesting that artists turn political. What I'm suggesting is that artists who are here for their independence should want to celebrate liberty because it is the only thing that enables you to express yourself freely. Those artists, those people need to know, like the left knows, when it's time to prop up a talking point or when it's time to turn something into a movement that is echoed in your art and then reflected in the politicians and their policies. Right now, the politicians are going to lead this conversation because artists on the right are too busy being blacklisted, feeling down on themselves, not feeling that anyone will will ever listen to them. And it's primarily because the response has typically been to make things more political instead of masking them in something really fun. The left is many decades ahead of the right in understanding this equation to the point where you can see and experience them abusing their power. It's their ability for the entire hive mind of the left to sing with one voice to dance in an organized fashion to get the point across in a way that is understood by people, which is not policy papers 50,000 words long explaining how things work. It's actually making people feel the way you want them to feel so that they will internalize the basic truth. And they won't forget it because people never forget the way that something made them feel but they always forget the other details. So the right gets suckered into focusing on details and trying to out prove who's smarter than the other guy who knows more of the intimate details of America's nuclear triad. What we need to do is we need to get inside the hearts and minds of audiences. That's how you wake people up. You don't wake people up by yelling to wake up to them. That just makes them close their eyes even harder. You do wake them up by waking up their spirit, waking up their heart, waking up their own self-awareness so that they can identify where they are in the story. And if you're running around with your own little community and your own little needs, you're not really in the full story. Instead you exist in an disorganized, manipulated, monetized chapter. Independent artists have to spread independence, and they have to do it in a way that is clever and smart enough to not be hitting the nail directly on the head. This is the big challenge for the independent movement of people who create content. Now you're going to start seeing more and more people go from social media to a television show or from Instagram to some contract player part on a series on Netflix. And all of this stuff is fake. Most of the people who go that path already have agents and managers and have already been discovered. It's a setup to set a false target for you to think that if you follow this path you might be able to make your dreams come true of having all the things you've ever wanted. But that's not where we're at right now. We're at a place where we have to be a little bit more brutally honest, and we have to really, really understand that all the things that you think you want are distractions. What you really want is order restored to the American way of life. Peace among our citizens. You want to be able to go outside and look at all of your neighbors and say, good morning instead of going outside and thinking that motherfucker voted for the other guy so I hate his guts. That's the system turning us on ourselves when it shouldn't be that way. And that great power, that great manipulation, that great ability the system has in one fell swoop to turn the story one way or the other is entirely dependent on the fact that the culture is completely owned by the left.

Here's my challenge to you, the independent creator. It is time to restore balance to the culture one side or the other should not dominate it, but it should be seen as a place where two sides of the story are told and embraced in a reasonable manner. We don't need to be divided by corporations to increase their profits when we can create beautiful, amazing, wonderful, inspiring, uplifting and hopeful art that is monetized and pays the artists directly and is supported by a public that understands the importance of keeping American culture alive. American culture truly is diversity that turns into a melting pot that unites us all around one true ideal that it is much better for man and woman to be free than it is to be subjugated by a tyrannical government. This is America. We pledge allegiance to the flag for which it stands, not the politicians for which we are told to sit down and hush up.

A FACE IN THE
CROWD

"I'll tell you exactly what's going to happen to you. You're going to be back on television only it won't be quite the same as it was before. There'll be a reasonable cooling off period, then somebody will say, why don't we try him again in an inexpensive format? People's memories aren't too long. You know, in a way, he'd be right. Some of the people forget, and some of them won't. Oh, you'll have a show. Maybe not the best hour or in the top 10. Maybe not even in the top 35, but you'll have a show. It just wont quite be the same as it was before, and a couple of new fellows will come along, and pretty soon a lot of your fans will be flocking around them. And then one day somebody will ask whatever happened to what's his name? You know, the one who was so big. Number one fella a couple of years ago. He was famous. How can we forget a name like that? By the way, have you seen Barry Mills? I think he's the greatest thing since Will Rogers._

That is the dialogue said by Walter Matthau's character Mel Miller to Lonesome Rhodes (a right wing political grifter played by Andy Griffith) in the final scene in the 1957 feature film A Face in the Crowd. A Face In The Crowd is an important film for a number of reasons. One, it that is was written by Budd Schulberg, son of BP Schulberg, one of the founders of Paramount Pictures. Budd was actively involved in the formation of the Writers Guild of America and got himself punched out by John Wayne in Puerto Vallarta, Mexico, specifically because John Wayne caught wind of the Communists organizing labor throughout Hollywood to solidify their business model of destroying classic American values through storytelling— values that are only useful to Hollywood when they're trying to build their brand and build their audience, which is the same reason they are promoting Communism now because their new audience is China. But this scene and this movie will destroy everything you know about modern punditry and pundits that you follow for political narrative. They are all based on this character of the famous political grifter who is too stupid to know that he's a tool of the corporations and not the other way around. The lefties have held this power from the beginning of the beginning, and they use it as a business model. This movie literally mocks every single person on the right and this scene in particular, is the moment the right has been told they're going into a media gulag and will be kept there. Furthermore the only people that the left will ever allow to reach the masses are people who maintain this divide who maintain this lie. And you, my friend, you, Mr. Rush Limbaugh, you will be quickly forgotten. That's what Matthau's character is saying. And it's true. You may think, *oh, this guy is crazy. I'm out of here. This book is stupid. Nobody can forget Rush Limbaugh.* Yes, they can. And they will, because the long game is much longer than your present reaction. The long game is much more important to the left than brand names. People who lionize personalities like like Rush Limbaugh do so at the peril of losing the entire country to the right wing culture con. What I'm telling you right now is the one reason Rush Limbaugh couldn't break out of that world he created, which looks big and significant and impactful and truly was to many of the people

I know. The reason he stayed just on those margins in the culture is represented right in the scenes pithy and truthful dialogue.

The left is more powerful than the right. The left is the power. The right has been co-opted to be the sort of adjacent power that keeps the left operational. We have to study A Face In The Crowd and we have to be OK with learning that the right wing political spectrum is a fix nothing fraud. It's OK to know the truth and it shouldn't change your political views. It doesn't change my views. What it changes, though, is our acceptance of being framed and pushed aside for embracing ammo, gold bullion and end of the world food supplies as these sort of like touchstones of an image of true patriotism that is so perverted from what it really is. This character-ization of the right is a kind of political narrative eye candy that draws us into their model, where the left then easily destroy us every single time. Look, the name of the game is a subversion, so we have to pretend to be on their side. We have to stop being so predictable. We have to value more than anything else our ability to change our mind. When we've been divided so cleverly and data backs up the divisions, we can destroy their di-visions by becoming completely unpredictable. That's why I say the greatest gift you have, the greatest tool you have is ideological inconsistency. Remember the truth about what you believe in? Your heart of hearts doesn't have to be reflected on the outside in this culture war. There's so many people I've met that outwardly don't look like they have the same values as I do. But when I sit down and talk to them, I find out we're almost iden-tical. And that's the primary negative effect of the balka-nization, the self balkanization by so many of us into our little battle corners. We don't talk to each other any-more and find out that we're actually identical but we have different ways of getting to the same point. And that's the conversation that, God forbid, we have because then the citizens might start to actually decide the way the country goes, as opposed to corporations, lobbyists and elites who have more assets than they know what to do with.

Look at Balkanized American culture like fish tanks that are sprinkled with agitating food so the elites can watch us all fight each other, sometimes to the death. Then they go and do the same thing to the next fish tank and the same thing to the next one. This moment has to be an earthquake for them. This moment has to be a time when the whole world shakes and all the fish tanks break. Because that's going to be the end of the left's game. They did this to themselves. They revealed their business plan, and they didn't even realize that it would come back to be used against them. That's what I'm trying to do here. Sub Pop Cult stands for Sub Pop Culture. We are the culture that is the real culture. The corporate one is fake. The truly indie subculture is real. The one that exists down at the street level. We're not going to be entrapped by shiny things and promises of vindication for our views. We're only going to be rewarded at the street level when we start sweeping our own streets, when we start taking care of things in our immediate world, when we start connecting with other human beings and not caring what their political view is. Because once we remove ourselves from the fake division, we instantly become so powerful that alarms go off in the halls of fame based power. Let's trigger every alarm. Let's make them truly panic, not the fake panic that they have their little minions point out, which is usually a tweet or something on social media that says, *they're panicking*—no, they will only panic when the American people speak with one voice and we speak with one voice when we ignore the one voice that divides us—the Mediadusa. Look into her eyes and your brain turns to stone.

THE ALGORITHM IS COMMUNIST

The world is run by computers, and those computers had to be programed by people. Embedded in the programing that the people gave computers is communism. The algorithm is communist and it intentionally creates all the divisions, all the heartache, all the anger and all the bitterness we feel towards one another because it is mined daily by you interacting with Google algorithms, Facebook algorithms and other algorithms that are out there for one purpose only, and that's to keep us divided. Who really knows what an algorithm is? It's not that complicated. It's a set of instructions. The most basic computer programing language that I learned in the early 1980s when I sat down at an Apple 2E was literally called Basic and there was a book that you could buy called I Speak Basic and it was written for children. Children could learn that programing is very basic instruction sets that says if this happens, then this should happen. If/then—those are the two words. So if the user presses this button, then the program has instructions to make the computer react this way or that way. Now just hold that thought for a second. That's the basic way that computer programing works and the basic way that an algorithm works. But an algorithm is different because the system is actually a hive mind now, and it controls all of society and scales upward until it's at the federal government level where everything is controlled by computer systems. There is a machine that bureaucrats feed human data into, and it spits back out potentially good policies or predictions on where things will go. Now those predictions, those results, it's all corruptible because data can be manipulated and the algorithm can manipulate it and get the results that it wants, the data that it needs to justify any policy. The algorithm exists outside of your physical reality. It exists in the place that you go and you interact with people or news articles on social media. I once heard from a friend that Ben Shapiro's success is due to him really knowing how to work the Facebook algorithm. That's impressive, I guess, unless you think about what it means to work the Facebook algorithm. It means taking advantage of the fact that the algorithm is constantly feeding the public aggravating stories because angry people click and people clicking is constant attention, constantly drawing more eyes to the show that they're watching, always reacting, constantly sharing and disseminating things that are absolutely useless to their own future which is floating by. But that's the algorithm. It keeps stimulating these interactions between us by feeding things to you that agitate the personality that you display every day by putting what you eat, what you've read, what you've watched, who you like, who you dislike, even the jokes. What's happening is the algorithm is overcoming the most powerful computer in existence: the human mind.

Consciousness itself is being reprogramed by all these divisive algorithms to react a certain way when it should be the opposite. The human mind should tell the algorithm what to do, and the algorithm should not be solely geared towards division, which creates clicks all day. Looking at Facebook all day, looking at Twitter all day, looking at something that has nothing to do with your physical life so that you can constantly give these people the fuel to sell advertising, to sell ad dollars, and also to cultivate in the people the qualities they want by way of a million digital paper cuts.

In 2012, I came across a book called The Idea Factory, Bell Labs and The Great Age of American Innovation by Jon Gertner. This book fascinated me because it taught me so much that I didn't know about the backbone of American technology and innovation. It has always been a government operation first and foremost. Very few people know that radar was invented by the folks who made up the original group of people that became Bell Labs. They worked out of a warehouse in lower Manhattan, and it was a major success that helped win WW2. Radar would not exist if it were not for Bell Labs and the men and women who worked there. When they moved to New Jersey is when the technology explosion occurred. The person who ran Bell Labs had a phone on their desk and it was a red phone, and that phone made one phone call. If it was picked up, it dialed the President of the United States, who kept close tabs on the innovations and work Bell Lab Labs was doing and it was a monopoly that eventually the government broke up its own monopoly and became Sprint and AT&T and all these different phone companies. But it all started consolidated at Bell Labs and those systems that they worked on were all about national security. That is what it was about and it still is to this day, but something very bad happened along the way. Something very strange occurred between Generation X and the generations that followed. Generation X was the last generation to see behind the computer screen, the last generation of people who were taught and encouraged to open the system and learn how it works by dismantling it and then rebuilding again. Everybody generation that followed has been given a mouse and a screen to point and click at and react to just the data. Data is like the skin of the body, but the organs are the hardware that enables the data to be presentable. And that's where the algorithm turned evil because it's no longer about giving you a tool to help you achieve your goals. Those things do exist. I use them. You use them. Everybody uses them. But the more powerful draw is that vaporware algorithm that encourages you to go one way or another with the way you live your life. It does produce the results in people that the system wants. Every single one of us is walking around with a human brain, and that brain can be programed as well. And it usually is by parents, the culture, families, and by schools. But that programing has turned against us while enough time and historical events have gone by that have distracted us from knowing that the algorithm exists and is running all interactions from behind, like a backseat driver. It's a dangerous time to be a free thinking individual because at the highest level of governments around the world, it has been decided that systems shall run humanity. The problem is systems lack humanity. They are impersonal server farms with algorithms that say, if the human does this, then direct them to that. And the only way to overcome destructive computer programing is with better programing. We're lucky, though, because we do have a computer program that was given to us that supersedes and overcomes the bad programing that inspires us to be pitted against one another. It is the word of God. When studied and pondered, when looked at and contemplated, is programing your mind to the true algorithm of human nature, the algorithm that it says if the person does this, then that will happen. It doesn't lie to you. It doesn't mislead you and it's never forced upon you because it is natural and hard wired into your being. This is the main reason why religion is under assault. It is the mystical computer program that is opposed to the evil human devised algorithms that nudge you into darkness.

The system wants to make the God algorithm into a farce because it's a problem for those who run the system, so they have to bastardize it and ruin its reputation. The word of God is the programing language of the human heart and mind. But the evil algorithm is a virus that has infected the human heart and mind, and when a virus infects the system, it can eventually takes it over. Think about your mind. Is it yours? Do you really own your thoughts, or are you constantly measuring your own thoughts and ideas against things that you see sent to you via the artificial programing language the algorithm created by failed men? Evil men. Men who would rather control and profit off your struggle than to see you flourish and reach your full potential. Now is the time to recognize that your brain is the most powerful unique computer in the universe and it networks with other powerful unique computers—your fellow human beings. We have our own algorithm in the form of traditions, community, the way we live our lives, inspired by and led by the word of God. All the things that we input create the good output. But if you allow yourself to be programed by the algorithms which serve profiteers of disunity, you only have to blame yourself for all the time that goes by with no progress and no peace. And the only thing you've left behind, your only legacy, is some snarky comments about political issues that passed and all you got was a lousy t-shirt. Don't let the algorithm hollow out who you are. Always maintain your character. Always maintain your peace. Always maintain your connection to the other human beings around you, and never let the abstract, obscure, hidden away algorithms of social media, government and show biz programs that do nothing but divide. You should never give in to that. It's a virus. Treat it that way.

AMERICAN APOLOGETICS

American apologetics is simply explaining the American way of life and clearing up some of the differences that we have so that people understand the simplicity of our methods for maintaining unity and purpose in a free world. The way to be a great American now is to forget about yourself. How does forgetting about the self restore American culture? It's pretty simple, because everything about American culture has recently been centered around self-service and the perversion of the American dream, which was never intended to be a story about going from rags to total riches to total domination of your fellow man. It was all about the story of going from nothing to something. The American dream coincides and parallels real life. You are born a nothing, and you become a something filled with knowledge, experience, love, truth, light, hard times, good times—all of it makes up your personal story, and in a modern society like the United States of America, we had established long ago that our unifying culture, our unifying rally around personal liberty was the one thing that mattered most and the thing that had to be defended at all costs to preserve the ability to reserve the option for Americans to be independently selfless.

Selfless Americans go about their business in pursuit of their happiness and pursuit of the joy of building something from the ground up that becomes a valuable company or a valuable product, or a valuable piece of information, but it all comes back to taking care of each other first to enable that journey for more and more, and it always has been. Only through media, through storytelling, through bad examples hammered into our head for many decades are we convinced that it's all about getting paid and having more than the other guy. It's the opposite of selflessness. It is extreme selfishness. And inspiring selfishness just so you can point to the system and say, see, this is what it inspires us—is a complete lie, a complete fraud. It's a manipulation that came after a long persuasion, and it's been seeded and planted in our culture for over time by diabolical people who know damn well what they've done and they've done it on purpose to destroy us. And you've heard me say this many times on my podcast—we the free people of the United States of America have the power to reverse this. It's going to take a wholesale adoption, a widespread embrace of selflessness in pursuit of preserving liberty.

Identity politics has been one of the most successful ways to increase selfishness in the American people for the purpose of nailing them to that cross and saying *"This is why your capitalistic system doesn't work."* Human nature tells us that people are going to abuse power and wealth no matter what. It takes a very, very strong willed person to avoid going down that path to avoid becoming their worst self. With this in mind, the selflessness of American culture prior to identity politics (which is successful because it makes people violently defend their vices and violently defend something that they've been told they can't have because other Americans don't want them to have it or do it.) was to resist being a part of something that is easily divisible against your fellow humans, your fellow Americans.

The selfless American society that I know wasn't one where everybody said, *"Your life has been unfair so let me give you everything that I have because you should have it and I shouldn't."* That's a lie. That's what people want you to think is selflessness, but it's actually not what it is.

10 percent is what tithe means. When you go to church, you would tithe 10 percent of what you earn. And the reason is this comes from an ancient practice of communities sharing their resources. If I was an apple farmer, I would donate 10 percent of my apples to the community so that people could have them. Somebody else would donate 10 percent of their lumber or 10 percent of their dairy products. And this was enabling people to grow exponentially by keeping the system going in a wholesome and just way that was good for all. And it enabled farmers, craftsmen, everyone to grow and grow and grow and become more successful. That's not communism that's caring for your community. Now, when the government uses all of its resources (and one of its resources happens to be Hollywood) when it uses all of its resources to cultivate in the people selfishness, part of it is so that it can come in and say, you're not caring about the community. And that's where the storyline is born, about community and groups and all these different camps of people that feel that they're not being cared for and they're not being represented. And why? Why is nothing happening the right way? Because we Americans adopted the reality that selfishness is capitalism and I'm going to defend my ability to be so selfish and fuck you if you don't understand. And the other side is, you're a fascist and you want to keep all the wealth and you don't want to help anyone and fuck you because you're a monster. And this is why communism is necessary now. Those are absurd, ridiculous points that we've been led by the nose to. And they're not at all reflective of what it's really like when American society

is humming along, when American society and culture is humming along and things are going well. It goes a little bit like this.

This Land Is Your Land by Woody Guthrie

This land is your land and this land is my land
From California to the New York island
From the redwood forest to the Gulf Stream waters
This land was made for you and me
As I went walking that ribbon of highway
I saw above me that endless skyway
Saw below me that golden valley
This land was made for you and me
I roamed and rambled and I've followed my footsteps
To the sparkling sands of her diamond deserts
All around me a voice was sounding
This land was made for you and me
When the sun come shining, then I was strolling
And the wheat fields waving and the dust clouds rolling
The voice was chanting as the fog was lifting
This land was made for you and me
This land is your land and this land is my land
From California to the New York island
From the redwood forest to the Gulf Stream waters
This land was made for you and me
When the sun come shining, then I was strolling
And the wheat fields waving and the dust clouds rolling
The voice come a-chanting and the fog was lifting
This land was made for you and me

The American spirit does not subjugate and dominate all people. The American spirit enables discovery, the journey, the walk. It enables the liberty and the freedom to go about walking across this land and knowing it's your land and my land, and that together we maintain its purpose which is freedom. We maintain the reality that although there may be walls with signs that say, keep out, there is nothing on the other side that is warning you of consequences. The American way of life is freedom. It is ignoring the sign that says keep out because nobody has the right to put it there. This doesn't mean that people can't have private property. This doesn't mean that security isn't necessary. This doesn't mean that you shouldn't have to lock your door. This doesn't mean that human nature disappears. But what it means is the American way of life in the American system is specifically about liberty existing beyond the wall. It shouldn't be there in the first place. That wall is metaphorical. The wall along the southern border is real, and it's part of the reason that the story of America is becoming perverted. We've let them build a wall to separate ourselves from everyone else, but this wall is real and will be used as a story device, and the disaster that always happens at the border is the most useful nonstop way to keep revisiting a problem that nobody wants to fix. Because this land is your land and this land is my land. But by putting a little hot button issues and setting up and physical spaces, they pervert the reality and they pervert the story so that the government can come in and be the mediator of liberty and be the one who knows they don't do their job of protecting America from foreign invasion or establishing baseline rules that we all have agreed to and voted for. No. Instead, they get involved in the narrative of America itself. The narrative that is only written by the people and their actions in the way they live their life and to change it and disturb it and mess it up and put walls over here and fake walls over there is all an attempt to take away that magical space that is on the other side of the do not enter sign. Americans are kind people and are generally very sincere. The sincerity reaches back to our ancestors and to the people who founded this country who cultivated in the people, the citizens of the country, qualities that would maintain liberty. The cultivation going on now are qualities that will undo liberty and the desire to defend it. Fight for it and realize that it is the last thing that is precious for it is the last thing that is truly American.

AMERICANISM

C ommunism has always been on the march, but only recently in modern history has it decided to march in broad daylight right down Main Street. There's only one remedy, there's only one system that beats Communism, and that is Americanism. If you think Americanism is bigger government, more progressive policies, more intrusion into the lives of private citizens—then you don't even know what country you live in, and if you think Americanism is access to as many guns as you can possibly fit into your basement, never having to come to any agreement with your fellow citizens over anything that infringes on your personal freedoms, then you don't know what it means to be an American. Both the left and the right have cultivated in the people the extreme expressions of our desires. People on the right who value and cherish personal liberty are coaxed into defending the most ridiculous versions of personal liberty. Things go viral like *what would you do if you found out your neighbor had a house full of weapons?* Things like that are counterintuitive. Everybody has a right to have a gun in the United States of America, whether you have 1 or 1000 is beside the point. But to get you to go out and really defend the access to a thousand guns in your home just for you, just in case, is just another way to have the narrative appear insane to the other side, the side that doesn't even know what country it lives in. And if you believe the freedom that America provides is really the freedom to convert America into a Communist system, you're expressing yourself in the most ridiculous way that inspires the other side to get a thousand more guns. The Second Amendment is what stands between the common man and tyranny. There is no doubt about it. It's been proven by what we've seen around the world during covid lockdowns in countries that are disarmed. But by having these ridiculous fights of the farthest possible left versus the farthest possible right, we never get a glimpse at what most of us cherish and experience every single day in our heart of hearts that we never want to go away. We don't really know what to call it, because nobody really understands what Americanism is anymore. It's been moved aside by slogans. It's been pushed away by politicians who rise in an internet media age. Every politician that takes you to an extreme stance in opposition to half the country, saying it's time to take the country back, has gone too far. There is no taking the country back from your neighbor. It's never going to happen. But there is taking the country back from the political class, and that will happen when enough Americans embrace Americanism, the system that beats Communism because it provides liberty for people to live their lives free and independently. We have to remember that we're all on the same team. The same team that has a player that dyes their hair purple, pierces every part of their body and only listen to music all day, has a teammate who wakes up at four in the morning to put on their work boots to go do a job that provides some service to their fellow citizens, providing some way of making life move forward. Both of these people are on the same team and dividing them against one another based on the way that they choose to live their life freely, is one of the great crimes that we've allowed to happen from the media to the people. And it's a crime because it's the tearing apart of the American family. It's the destruction of Americanism, leaving the only place left to go after you destroy Americanism is right into the hands of Communism.

AMERICAN JOUST

The medieval joust has its origins in the military tactics of heavy cavalry during the High Middle Ages. By the 14th century, many members of the nobility, including kings, had taken up jousting to showcase their own courage, skill and talents. And the sport proved just as dangerous for a king, as a knight, and from the 15th century on, jousting became a sport without relevance to warfare. And just like any modern sport, the joust created a great metaphor for how to be on the same team, but also fight over things. The difference between now and then is now the public and citizens who are far from power are encouraged to fight to the death, while those who are in leadership positions and have their thumbs on power know that they are engaged in a joust with each other. They're on the same team because they play towards the same end, however, they don't hit each other with real swords, but they're always asking you and I to murder each other in the name of ideological purity. There is not one person who can reasonably say that the media does not manipulate the citizens of the United States specifically, and they manipulate us so that we don't have this revelation that we can we fight over something but remain on the same team and understand that you win some, you lose some and to be happy for the other guys win, even if you're losing. This can only happen in a mindset that knows when you lose you haven't been killed, you've only been knocked off your horse temporarily.

As free citizens of the United States of America who have correctly identified that we are oppressed by media narrative storytelling that divides us against one another, there is an opportunity for us to overturn the system by a series of steps and one of the first steps, the thing that I've been trying to cultivate the most in the audience of my podcast, is resisting the reaction to sensational news, but also resisting fighting to the death over trivial things. We can establish the American joust where we all know that our teams are clear. There's the haves and the have nots, and the have nots outnumber the haves by a massive margin. And the have nots are not poor people. There are people who have not understood the media manipulation and have not been related to the system in a way that benefits them at all financially. And the haves are those who have their fingers on the levers of culture and power and influence so they can establish in us the instantaneous reaction, the sarcastic reaction, the thing that we shouldn't do, they have us in a situation where we exist as political hemorrhoids. You add the ingredient from this topic with the juxtaposition of something that doesn't make sense and all hell breaks loose. That's that distracting that prevents us from engaging in the American joust. Instead, we should all understand this very true thing about life: you're not going to be here forever and you can't take it with you. You can't take the gold and treasure with you. You can't take the sarcastic memes with you. None of that travels with you beyond this world. So while you're here, why do you play for keeps? Why do we, as competitive individuals in the United States of America, take the bait and play for keeps as if our government is not one diabolical institution that pretends to be two sided? It's us against the government, and the government has completely fooled everyone, even the most sophisticated folks who believe what they're doing is saving the country or saving democracy or restoring order but no matter who you elect you get the government. And no matter what you do, we're still We the People, and we need to recognize that and remember it and participate in the American joust and knock each other off our horses, but then get up and shake hands. The more we do that, the more we don't take the bait and dive into deep, permanent divisions that seem unsolvable—the more we joust and get up and joust again and are happy for the guy who wins and helping the guy who got knocked off his horse—we'll create a harmony among ourselves that will be more powerful than any top-down government persuasion campaign, inspiring you to drive a sword through your fellow American's heart. Take those swords and put them away. Pick up the lance and joust. But when the government comes to intercede, pick the sword up again and say, *You shall not cross here. This is our space. This is our sovereign territory where we joust and build our future together.* And the future that we're building has no dependency on the current reality. The future we're building is dependent on us staying united and moving forward so that we can jettison the personalities and the people who have been front and center of our political disaster for the past 50 years.

The Mediadusa

Everything that can be manipulated will be manipulated and everything that can be programed will be programed, believe it or not, you are manipulatable and programable. And that's exactly what's happening with American culture. This is by design. If you've been listening to my podcast and paying attention to the things I've told you, you realize that the media has a script as well. Their script is very complicated, but it does go on a time frame, and it does serve the needs of corporations, politicians, elites and people who own media companies. The last thing they can do is have us tune out because if we tune out, they have no power anymore. It's that simple. Nobody's going to come to your house, knock on the door and pull you away. Nobody's going to stop your car, demand you to pull your sleeve down so they can jam a needle into your arm. That's not going to happen. There's going to be situations where people are told if you want to come to work, you have to get vaccinated or you need to get tested regularly because it's a government incentivized moneymaking bonanza. The Government always knows how to get what it wants whenever it wants.

Think about marijuana. A long time ago, marijuana was legal. It was a commodity. It was farmed. It was no big deal at the time the government decided to eradicate it. How did it achieve its goal? Government said, If you would like to grow marijuana, fine, you just have to get stamps from us at the federal government and those stamps will represent a certain number of crops that you can grow. What the government did is they never made the stamps. So everybody got kind of caught holding nothing. Government got what it wanted when it wanted. Think about covid, where for most people it was just cheaper and easier to get vaccinated. The stated goal has always been (f you listen to the information that is not directed at your anger point, but is always embedded deep inside every article that you never read) that the goal has always been for every man, woman and child to acquire COVID-19 one way or another—some version of the Delta variant or the social media variant, it doesn't matter what it is, everybody has to get it so that herd immunity can be established. Now, the real thing that happened here and this is not even debatable, is herd immunity in this case has been monetized. It's been turned into a money making opportunity even though it would have happened naturally. People would have been sick in large numbers but there would have been no profit margin there. Now there is. You got your vaccine. Now come get your booster. Now, come get your next booster. Now, how about another booster after that? And that is all transactional. Someone has to pay for it. Some federal government or state agency has to purchase the vaccines. We're talking hundreds and hundreds of billions of dollars made by companies that wouldn't have made any if herd immunity had worked the natural way. I am a germaphobe and I am somebody who is very cautious about touching my face, my eyes, sticking my finger near my mouth. When I'm out, I wash my hands chronically, doing what I can to take care of myself so that I'm not spreading germs to myself from contaminated surfaces that are touched by others.

That's really the highest risk for getting colds in general. You learn that pretty quick when you're a parent and you send your children to their first couple of years of school, they bring home every germ and virus that ever existed on planet Earth and it destroys and then inoculates the adults. You come out of it by the time they're in seventh grade and you're immune to most stuff. It's true. A parent told me that at the beginning of my young child's life, and now that she is a teenager in high school we have gotten sick less than anybody we know that doesn't have children over the last five or six years. So there is something good to being exposed, which is very, very helpful to your health. The other factor is your body has to learn to fight viruses. If you take the vaccine because you choose to, that's fine. But what you're doing is you're weakening your body's natural immune response. Now they will tell you everything they can to nudge you, to frighten you, to scare you, into getting the jab. They want you on the program to maintain this new money making precedent.

Speaking of precedent, what about those yearly flu shots? For most people your body will get the flu and will learn to combat that version of the flu, and you get that much stronger. So really, a vaccine is like a remote control and you're asking somebody to go and change the channel for you. And if you do that long enough, you allow your immune system to metaphorically sit on its ass and become out of shape, become immobilized, become dependent on the remote control, you'll get sicker every time you do catch something. So for young people, people like myself who are in a very healthy category, eat right, get enough exercise and vitamin D, all of those things—I just prefer to have my body learn to fight things the natural way. What I want is my body to learn, to identify and have those white blood cells attack seasonal viruses and make my immune system work for me the way it was designed by God, who also equipped every human being with an immune system that detects bullshit. It's called the ability to reason the ability to think through and consider options and come to some conclusion that is closer to the truth than the lies. This is an interesting comparison to the way vaccines work because getting exposed to the germ itself, the virus itself, will give you a stronger ability to fight it in most cases and a more likely long term resistance to it if you are lucky. But getting the vaccine, as I just established, is like a shortcut for most people. Not for people in high risk categories, but for most young people who don't need that remote control. It is a shortcut, so how do we shortcut our way away from reason and defer it to other people? It happens on social media where you let others think for you and you simply say to yourself, *you know, that sounds right*, and then you hit share, or then you go and spread that word that you heard that sounded right to you, to somebody else in public. And that is the that is the dirty little seed of misinformation and how it's spread around. So how do you vaccinate yourself against that without actually taking extreme measures like some kind of a shot? What would the metaphor be for a shot, a shot that inoculates you against social media misinformation would be not to be exposed to social media. It would be to mask up your social media and not look it in the face anymore. It would be to recognize that the media is really the Mediadusa and when you look into her eyes, your brain turns to stone. There's no more thinking, there's no more reasoning. There is no more using your mind's ability to consider all options and determine what is closest to the truth. And it's because social media, just like the remote control, has made us lazy thinkers. We have others think for us and we just say, I approve. And we adopt it, but if you go about your everyday life, you are forced to think for yourself out in public and what happens when you're out in public, you make decisions. None of those decisions are as extreme or dramatic as the opinions and talking points that are spoon fed to you by professional pundits who really have no skill in this world but simply want the attention and the accolades and the potential for making a good amount of money, doing a very little amount of real work. It's a scam that only elites know because they've created it but you can participate in it, and you can scam the elites right back. You can scam them the first way, by ignoring them, because that's all it is. You have popular social media personalities walk into the middle of a staged circle and they say, *Look at this crazy thing that I'm doing, look at this crazy thing that this person is doing.* Everybody reacts to it because it is crazy. But the conversation topic is not yours. It's never yours. So make the conversation yours, no matter who you are, no matter what you believe—make it yours. And don't listen to anybody else. If we all start talking our own truth (and I mean, really, our own truth, like the person in the inner city who wakes up and he has to deal with an extreme violent situation outside their door) that person should be able to tell us that truth without it being spun in a political matter. But just the matter of fact that *there's danger out my door and this is unacceptable. I have small children and I'm trying to raise them up and get them out of this situation instead of that turning into a political talking point, you know?* Whenever you see something like this, whenever somebody does voice a concern like this, it's quickly put away and instead it's turned into something that is more expedient towards the political class. And it all revolves around their collective grasp on national narrative. This fact is a very important thing for you to dwell on because it's all storytelling and you're an author as well and you're also the star of your own show but to the system you're actually the product and the product that you are is a trail of data that you leave behind that tells companies everything they need to know so that they can manipulate and program you according to their ends.

You are just a mark, you are just a dot. You are not a human being with a heart, with feelings, with emotions, concerns and cares and dreams, you are data on their page. So we have to change the data because that's what they will react too. When the data says that none of the people want this anymore and none of the people are participating in this narrative anymore, the narrative will change. And when they don't have a replacement for it, like this moment right now, the narrative will change to being the narrative of the people, by the people and for the people because sidelined creators are liberated and there has never been a time like now to communicate with one another. Share what is true. Disseminate what is false. Think for yourselves and get the best out of social media that we can get as individual people connecting with other people who can help you reach out and try to make things happen together. I've done that, and most of the contacts that I've met through social media that I've followed all the way through into real life have turned into excellent contacts, people that I can work with. So a lot of the media distractions are preventing those moments from occurring and preventing Americans from connecting. Don't let the storytelling bullies stand in the middle of your future connections that will help you reach your goals. Everybody is out there trying, so break through the conversations, break through the lies and have a breakthrough in your own life by living your narrative, speaking your truth, doing so in such a way that doesn't serve politicians, but communicates to your fellow Americans that this is what life is like for me and here's why you should care, and here's why we should work together to improve it for all. And really, it doesn't have much to do with the government as mediator, it has everything to do with us and how we feel about each other. Reestablishing our story of liberty, reestablishing our individuality and restoring in the

minds of the world, the truth about who we really are—
free people who are free to make decisions and free to
think and free to love one another. As soon as we are
wise enough to turn away from the manipulation and
turn off the media and turn to one another and start
building the future that we all want, the sooner the divisions will end.

THE AMERICAN SENSE

Most humans are born with five senses that are in working order. They are sight, smell, hearing, taste and touch. Sometimes people are born without those senses working at all. People are born blind, deaf and sometimes have to rely only on the sense of touch to understand what the world might look like. But the one sense that all humans are born with that every created creature who walks this planet is imbued with is the religious sense. The religious sense is the calling of the mystery of God, into the truth, into what things truly mean about your existence and how you fit into the universe. But that can only be expressed in a system and a place that has been established not so long ago so that mankind may be free to explore his religious sense. And it all depends on the American sense, the sense of Americanism that is born into all of us and also calls those from around the world who want to be part of our wonderful nation of free people. How many times have you watched the news or read the stories of violence only to have the author of a story or the host of a news program complain that Americans are desensitized to violence, desensitized to murder, desensitized to corruption, desensitized to pedophilia, desensitized to everything. But truly, the thing we are desensitized from

is our American identity. It gets lost in the confusion. It
gets shuffled in the deck and hidden like the Joker, when
really it's the Ace card and the Ace card is something
that you are born with if you are lucky enough to be
born in America. It's our job as citizens to help each
other maintain the American sense, that unique ability
to see liberty for what it truly is. To feel freedom in its
true capacity. The wisdom to hear the lies embedded in
the stories in the news that takes us away from our own
American culture.

The joy of experiencing different cultures in the true
authentic way is through food. Food tells the story of a
people and those stories come to America and become a
part of our diverse tapestry of cultures. And they have a
specific taste which reflects the specific people who concocted it through history. But the most important sense,
the sense that we have collectively seemingly lost touch
with is the ability to sense bullshit. I'm not talking
about manufactured political bullshit put upon you so
that you'll have a reaction. I'm talking about bullshit
embedded in the narrative that divides us because we are
divided by bullshit. It's the American sense, the ability
to see and understand and taste and smell and experience the gifts of liberty as they are established in the
United States of America really relies on your ability to
see through and smell the bullshit. It stinks really bad
right now because we are drowning in it. There's a
whole industry of bullshitting us to keep us divided.
This is the thing nobody really wants you to know because lots of people are incentivized to take advantage of
the bullshitting system. But enough time has gone by
and enough people have been hurt that we're all starting
to collectively sense something is diabolically wrong
with the way our government treats us and deals with us
as a free people. Freedom is slipping away, but only we
can reel it back in and place it in the center of our lives.
In the center of our beings. And it all involves the Amer-

ican sense being nurtured and cared for by you, the individual and then making sure that your friends and your neighbors also have the same sense so that we can look past the cloud, we can look past all the noise, we can look past the smoke and the mirrors so we can still see one another and we can still understand this precious gift we have. Know that an evil globalist world would like to rob the American citizens of that precious gift that our founding generations fought and died for.

Many years ago, I was in a conversation with an actor. He told me a story about his dad. We were really complaining about the lack of common sense in the people around us when we were working on a project and he said, *"my old man told me, if it's so common, how come more people don't have it?"* It was a good point, and I think of it to this day, and that's why I realize that desensitization of the American Sense is really what's behind all the confusion. If you have a sense of well-being, if you've established a home and some healthy ways that you live—that sense of independnet well-being is what people want. The sense of being free is also what people want. And it used to be common because both were embedded in our culture, in our stories, in the things we celebrated, in the people we elevated to the top so that we could celebrate their achievements and also use them as examples to show the great common sense of Americanism and the American way. But that is missing now, and that missing common sense creates a situation that is exactly like what happens in a human being who has one sense of theirs not working at full capacity. The other senses overcompensate and work even harder and help define the individual. So in this case, the American sense is missing, and therefore there's an opportunity to fill that with identity politics, where people can find a sense of belonging. The American sense is a sense of belonging to one nation under God, indivisible with liberty and justice for all. But after about a decade of people being encouraged to self balkanized into special interest groups, it's been very easy using the algorithms of social media to pit us against one another so that we fight winless battles. That's what I said in the very first episode of my podcast is—the world of culture in America was Balkanized, and the Balkanization allows the different groups to be pitted against each other. So keep this in mind when you work on refinding your American sense—division equals the destruction of us, unity equals the destruction of they/them. So keep your American sense sharp at all times. Learn how to use your five senses to experience the true American life with your eyes. You will see different people living their life according to their desires and with your ears you will overhear conversations about hopes and dreams that people have for their future and with your mouth you can taste the food from the different cultures that come to America and make up our diverse landscape. And with your hand, you can reach over and shake the hand of your fellow American and start a friendship rooted in common sense. The common American sense that it is better for mankind to be free from tyranny and to have a government that is of the people and by the people and for the people, and that our culture is one of freedom and we agree as a nation of independent, free thinking, diverse different people that at all costs freedom must be preserved.

BAPTISM BY LIARS

It feels like the world has turned upside down. In fact, we all refer to it as the upside down. The reason we refer to it as the upside down is because of a television series called Stranger Things. I'm not writing about Stranger Things to promote a television series. I'm here to explain to you today that the audience is always created before the product, the product in this case, in the bigger picture, is government rule exclusively and the end of organized religion. This is a frightening prospect if you look at it and you think about it because all that's happening through culture, is young people are experiencing a baptism by liars, which converts them into compulsive, pathological sociopaths—the perfect type of personality who will always work as a minion for those in power to increase worldliness among their fellow human beings and decrease any relation they have to a mystery that is above and beyond corporations and dollars and cents. This baptism by liars draws you down into the depths of darkness, where you sink to the bottom and you don't know what happened. You fall so far down that the light you wish could find, you may not be able to see because the storytelling layers are so thick and the lies are so convincing.

First let's unpack how layers of storytelling create

markets and reality. I'll use an example that's probably fresh in the memories of many people who listen to my weekly show. Saving Private Ryan was a big, ambitious World War Two movie directed by Steven Spielberg. The subject of WW2 at the time was not mainstream and popular with anyone under 70. Dreamworks studio leveraged The History Channel and the Discovery Channel audience to achieve creating interest in WW2. So if you're making a movie for an audience that doesn't yet exist you have to create one ahead of time to justify the high cost of making the entertainment in the first place. The way that this is done is in the year or two before Saving Private Ryan came out, there was lots and lots of TV shows and books about the greatest generation, WW2 and general themes that matched the upcoming movie, which is getting you interested in a time frame and a storyline that you weren't previously paying attention to at all. This is developing the audience slowly and preparing their mind as fertile ground for that seed to be planted, which produces this fruit: you're going to go buy tickets to this movie and you're going to take everybody you know with you. That is how show business works—audiences are created before product, and the reason is making the product is so expensive that you have to justify it and everything is justified using data. So they all put out programs to browbeat you into being the perfect consumer for what they're making. And after you watch the programs by tuning in, they'll have the data to back it up that says the audience exists. With the collapse of the movie business being official, with Barry Diller coming out and announcing it's over, the movie business will never come back to the way it used to operate. Don't misinterpret that as the end of show business or the end of entertainment because it's not. As a matter of fact, the corporations which are armed with all the money and all the ability to reach consumers, are interested in increasing their baptisms by liars so that they can get more and more and more people to become Avon sales ladies for worldliness. But there is an opportunity here to take advantage of something else that was created, possibly unintentionally, but we all see it and we all know it's sitting right there, which is this—media corporations thought they were creating Balkanized audiences to increase their profits. You have the LGBTQ community, you have liberals, you have right wingers, you have all kinds of people divided up into this hodgepodge of competing ideologies, essentially always some iteration of left versus right or too much government versus too little government, anarchists over here and authoritarians over there. It's just ridiculous chaos. A 24/7 orgy of political narrative nonsense. And that's exactly how the worldliness crowd likes it because it increases their ranks. But it also creates a new audience very slowly, which is now at it's tipping point and that is an audience desiring something true, something peaceful, something that reflects the upward desire to be better than we are, to be better than our conflicting human nature. To be above human nature is not something that is possible, but to aim above human nature is practical, and it is a tool that is a bedrock part of all religion. When you go to church, you're really saying, *I'm checking out of the world and its culture for this time, and I'm going to sit here and be reminded and worship the true things that were given to me by God and presented to me by the Son of God.* For us Christians, when we go to church that's what we're doing. We're checking out of the world for a day. It's a way to just, you know, let pages of your life story go, just say, OK, that was a chaotic week with a lot of craziness and a lot of violence and a lot of hatred. But I'm checking out of it today. I'm turning the page and going to remind myself to stay connected to this mystery that inspires me to try to be better than my nature. The baptism by fire leads you to this moment, because there's been some great disappointment, some great turmoil, something that has shifted your vision so that you actually glimpse the truth. But it's very, very hard for many people who are surrounded by the baptism by liars crowd, the people who tell them that it's a virtue to be one way or the other when it's actually destructive to the whole country.

There is a viral video that has gone around the internet many times of Frank Zappa talking about what went wrong with art in the United States, how it turned corporate in the most ironic way possible. When the record business was corporate and arbitrary and run by out of touch suits that didn't care about the content, they just cared what sold and what didn't, you had much better music that really represented the wide tapestry of opinions and ideas that make up American life in American culture. But once you have middlemen who have moved in and made themselves the star of the show in the form of star producers, famous talent agents, legendary managers, these folks have egos bigger than the talent that they represent. And the reason they do is because they're playing chess with movie stars and pop-culture. They're moving actors and personalities and entertainment across the board, and they're celebrating their cultural wins while fattening their pockets at the same time as draining peace and happiness from American life. If we remove these guys from the equation (the middlemen) where they don't even belong (they should be fetching artists coffee) then artists in the new creator economy will become an absolute necessity to rescuing America's culture. We will begin to get things that are true again. We will have songs about true love. We will have movies that show the true struggle. We will have literature that tells the truth about human nature and its constant ability and desire to overcome itself and all other obstacles. We will get the truth put back into our culture. The truth that is missing and it's only missing because a group of punks wedged themselves in between the content creators and the content distributors and they balkanized the audience and made it profitable for themselves. And they all became culture puppeteers, the highest paid puppeteer says *I have my hand on the pulse. I'm pulling all the strings. Look what I can do.* That business model has run its course. And the only way back to peace, happiness, truth and beauty is when we the people begin to tell our stories to one another and we embrace each other's stories for what they are—the American experience communicated directly from one person to the next. So check out of politics and tune in to each other. That's how we restore American culture.

IN ONE EAR

The second inning of the current political narrative began shortly after Joe Biden took office. The second inning, as you know, because you're still stuck in the middle of it now, is about distracting the right with nonsense so that the right wing media personalities will lead you to the proper reaction, which then prevents you from ever acquiring power by organizing and getting focused like a laser beam on the things that truly matter. Deep down you know what truly matters is right outside your front door. And you know, what does not truly matter is the storylines that we are led to embrace by both sides of the political elite working hand in hand to share their access to the gold coins sitting in the middle. They don't want you to have them. They don't want me to have them. And they don't want anyone new to innovate a new way to do anything because once you have control of Government systems that work for you, you're in the driver's seat of an easy life of luxury and all that you need to do to prevent anyone from taking that from you is to distract them. That is the name of the game. That's what people do in professional life as well.

There are two kinds of people you'll encounter in your professional life. You'll encounter the person who really does care about cultivating the people who are going to come after them and helps them rise up through the ranks. And you'll encounter the type who identifies talented folks who, whether it's in film or business or any line of work, is essentially a threat to the status quo, so they preoccupy and mislead the younger generations new talent because the power is consolidated and they don't want the younger generation to replace them. These types seek to train the younger generations to maintain the system as it is now, with They/Them in charge. The system is heavily dependent on consumers. And America has always been the consumer class that decided so many things globally based on our buying power that has been offset and taken from us and moved over to China. The Chinese people now have that power to decide the way fashions, trends, all the things that were American made in the past that were intellectual in nature are corrupted or gone. So we don't have manufacturing and we don't have cultural power. Our elites have sold out the country. So what can we have? What are we left with? We're left with each other. That's it. But that is a lot because it's everything. Me and you working together to build a better world is so much more powerful than me and you reacting to the lies that both sides put out so competition will spin its tires in mud. But the difference between We the People and They/Them, the Government elites, is how we define the future. When the left, the organized group of people that consists of leftists and folks who call themselves conservative when they work together to divide us away from our real true goals that would help us, it's because they have another definition of what a better future will be. That definition is always something that they can manage and monetize That's what it is. It's *we need to prioritize this marginalized group and put them on top because they used to be on the bottom* and it enables they/them the ability to manage and control something over time. The government is essentially a meddler that gets into the people's business, creates problems that weren't there before so that it can provide the solutions. Government meddling wasn't something that was so prevalent not too long ago. And the reason is culture has significantly changed. We all talk about woke culture, and we all talk about people who are too sensitive. I am part of Generation X, and when I was a child, we used to say *sticks and stones may break my bones, but names will never hurt me.* But we also used to say, *let it go in one ear and right out the other.* That was a culturally normalized habitual way of reminding us not to hold onto the things that are bothersome and also not to be bothered by things that aren't truly problems. Because if you think about it, sticks and stones may break our bones but names will never hurt us. It is true. So how did the government meddle through media to make it so that names will actually hurt people? I know sophisticated, intelligent adults who get attacked on Twitter and feel the assault of words, almost proving that what we used to say is not true, but it is true and these folks have been conditioned to care so much through the culture and through storytelling that succeeded in creating a victim class. You're forced to participate in that narrative when you really don't have to. You can say anything you want and even if it's negative and it can be the most ridiculous thing of all—racist, hateful, it doesn't matter. It's still just words and it shouldn't hurt anyone.

Why is everyone so afraid of words? Because words, as the left knows, become thoughts that then turn into action. So they have rained down all these words to create all these victims, and the evidence is clear. It's worked. Storytelling has created a victim class and a victim class is this generational group of people who are literally shaking in their boots, sometimes by what somebody has said, a total stranger even. That's bizarre to me. Now, if someone comes running at you with a baseball bat, that's different. That's an aggressive form of assault that is going to hurt. But if someone says your racial name or they attack your sexuality or whatever, that's meaningless and everyone knows it and it has no power or no impact whatsoever. Words don't really do anything to people but they do motivate them to positive action when used correctly and destructive action when this power is abused. And so because we've been cultivated into this victim class, the words that are the opposite of the victim class have a special weight now and they have a special importance and they suddenly feel like they're necessary. That's just one of the ways that I think they draw us into being radicalized without being truly radicals because true radicals would put their nose to the grindstone and figure out how to overturn a system that lies to both sides. But to be radicalized is to echo the insanity that both sides want you to so the problems increase and the government can provide the solutions. We're suckers. We have to stop being suckers. It's not hard. Face the music. We've been duped over and over again, and a terrific way to become un-duped is to return to the sayings that stimulate the right thought inside someone's mind. The a reason why we're so agitated now is because everything goes in one ear but it never goes out the other. It goes in one ear and it's added to the other lie and then another lie goes in one ear and they all build up in your head until you explode with rage. That explosion based on lies would never happen if somebody unclogged the drain and things went in one ear and out the other. Let's repopularize the idea that sticks and stones may break our bones, but names shall never hurt us. And all things that are said that are negative, they will go in one ear and out the other so that they don't collect and poison our collective brains. It's a survival instinct that has been taken away through diabolical storytelling. The sticks and stones tradition has been moved aside, but it still exists and it's still true.

Have two people stand across from each other in a boxing match shouting names and obscenities at one another and let me know when someone's knocked out. Let me know when somebody is stumbling around and they can no longer stand up and think for themselves because of what has been said to them. If somebody does behave that way and we've seen the videos of "Karens" freaking out on everybody and acting emotionally distraught—just remember that we do have a mental illness problem in this country. So you can take every mental situation you find, line those videos up and spoon-feed them to the public and make them think there's an epidemic when there isn't. These people need to be told *get up, they're only words that you should let them go in one ear and out the other.* That's what we have to do with every lie. You should have a filter in your brain, and the the other side automatically opens when it's not something beneficial and true. You just let it out, let it go.

RETURN OF THE COOLER

My goal with my weekly podcast and now this book, is to raise you up as an organized group of independent creators, all acting in your own self-interest, creating and restoring the culture that is missing from the United States. We are being drowned in corporate culture driven by corporate story-telling that is only about getting you to buy more products and become a better customer. We need unity. We need peace. And we need love among ourselves. We're never going to get that if we keep tuning in to the shit show, which divides us among the most basic, ridiculous traits you can possibly find in human beings. Divided we fall is true for families, for relationships with individual people and for governments and for the health of an entire nation. It is one of the truest things that is said about the United States, but it's true for everybody. If your family is fractured and broken, somewhere in time the division took hold and grew. If your country is fractured, it's a little different. The division was planted and encouraged to grow by diabolical government officials who benefit from the division. The division in this country has been monetized for a long time. I think a lot of people on the right generally feel very, very, very duped by our political class, which claims to represent us. They don't. They represent their own self-interest, and they use the pre written storylines of left versus right as the backdrop to perform and please constituents with a little bit of theater, a little bit of talk, but no action. And this is made possible by clever writers of political narrative, particularly headlines that use words that really paint a picture in your head like something is happening. How many times have you read that the politician that you support has slammed the politician that you dislike? Or how many times have you read that the politician you dislike has ripped the politician that you like? Using these words to create pictures of actual combat happening between each of them is an advertising tactic. It's a way of implanting in your mind an inception that these people are really fighting each other because the truth is, the news is quite boring otherwise. Government is quite boring and a lot of these efforts that these folks put on, I'm starting to believe, is for their own ego so that they feel they're not doing something that is totally boring. Government should not be this exciting place where all these dramatic fights happen and then the stars move from their elected position to being Netflix producers and getting big book deals and seven figures to explain to us how they governed into deeper division. This marriage between show business and government is absolutely poison and it seems like we'll never get over it because elected officials are human too, which means they are flawed. I can tell you in humble honesty that if you take a blue collar kid like me and you give me too much wealth and too much power, I don't think it would be very difficult for me to turn into a diabolical, weird person that is completely out for my own self-interest. It's part of our human nature. You have to know this about yourself to avoid it, and this brings me to one of the revealing things about all of our elected officials—they seem to have no self-awareness whatsoever. It's almost as if they don't want to try to see what they look like to the rest of us. They want to talk down and tell us how we should see them and frame the conversation for us. And it's easy to do because it's not just government officials, it's their friends in corporate show business who edify whatever message needs to be edified to move the consumer base in whichever direction is beneficial to the elites, and we give them this free pass by playing along. What we should do is turn it around and we should first start by telling them *we've had enough of you projecting your duties onto us. We elected you to handle politics. We didn't elect you to spoon feed political narrative to us and then monetize our battles and turn us into competing audiences with separate marketplaces, separate iPhones, separate currencies, separate everything, divided and fallen.* This division is a corporate division. It is America, the corporation, and it got too big and too powerful and some people in the world said, *hey, it's time to break up that corporation.* That's why our government never breaks up the companies, the companies just keep breaking up the people instead. This is only possible because we all agreed to meet at the digital water cooler.

A long time ago in the 1970s the office water cooler was the place where people in the professional world shared opinions on what entertainment or politician they liked, and that was how word of mouth got spread. Or what sports team they liked or who died or what happened nationally and how it impacts them locally. The water cooler was the place where people intersected in small numbers, I'm sure one or two at a time. Bob and Steve or Karen and Jeff both end up at the water cooler. They talk a little bit about life, the weather, politics. Did you read that new book? Did you see that show? That was a much milder and truly localized and therefore a true experience because it was decentralized narrative dissemination. It wasn't part of a network that could be manipulated. There wasn't anybody who could suddenly change water cooler conversations one direction or the other based on lies. It was the place where opinions were shared among citizens. So it's a really good metaphor for how the system can work at a local level, but now all water coolers are connected by the internet and everything that is said is heard by the internet, instantaneously shared, instantaneously manipulated. One billion people step up to the water cooler at the same time and they say. *I don't like this policy.* Well, the water cooler responds now and it changes the conversation to whatever it wants. This is what's happening in our government and our media and the public unknowingly plays along. The strongest thing we have (and I say it a lot because I mean it) is ideological inconsistency in the face of a data collecting system. It's a true necessity right now. You have to be willing to say the talking points of both sides whenever necessary. And by the way, if you do this, you'll start to see that is all they are—mere talking points. If somebody challenges you and is trying to pick a political fight, you just tell them *I believe in exactly what you believe in* because the goal here is to put everyone's fire out so that we can focus. Our goal as free people shouldn't be to violently overtake the system and participate in the theatrical bloating of reality into something that it's not. Our goal should be to collectively manipulate the system to behave how we want it to behave. Because that's what the system does to you and I, it manipulates our behavior so that it benefits the system. I believe that independent creators can be the force that corrects this. I believe that when people in their own self-interest tell their stories and share them with the world in an independent marketplace that is embraced by Americans who know we have to restore our culture, that culture change will follow. It's not corporate culture. It's something different. It's very unique because it's so diverse and it all melts into one thing, namely, the American reality. We need to do this to change the dynamic to reverse the equation.

There's a lot of talk and a lot of excitement about blockchain technology and the ability to have transparent accounting. Transparent accounting for independent creators who put their creations on a blockchain system that allows audiences to access it and download it will experience the greatest transfer of wealth from media companies to artists that ever happened. And when enough artists are successful in this new marketplace, more and more will choose to go the independent route over going and soliciting their work to a major corporation that is probably not going to buy it, is likely to steal it, and even more likely to cut them out of the equation to the lowest possible share. So this is how the culture is going to get changed. This is how America is going to reunite when we start re-embracing our roots, re-embracing our old folktale way of telling each other stories about American life. Folk filmmakers are out there, independent musicians are out there. There's people doing what they can with what they have now. We, as audience members, have to join them in celebrating this and making it into a truly massive underground movement. There's off-Broadway and there's pop culture and then there's sub pop culture. That's what I'm trying to create here with your help. Sub pop culture doesn't sell anything (besides this book) It doesn't ask you to subscribe, it doesn't market things to you, but it is trying to plant an interception into all the young minds that are reading this to embrace your independence. Embrace this young period in your life. You don't really need a massive health care package. You don't need all these different expensive things when you're just an 18 year old kid, healthy, fortunate to live in a free country and have the tools at your disposal to create content and deliver it to audiences and change the world. That's the mission. It's a young man's job. It's a young woman's job. It's a young person's job. Young people have to do this. You have to dig in and take back the United States from corporations aiming to destroy our identity as the melting pot. It's one of the real take backs that needs to be done. When politicians are saying, *join me and we will take back our country*, they never mean it. They always mean *join me in this theatrical pretend take back of our country, but really sit down and shut up once I'm elected. And then go away.* Truly taking back the country is taking it back through culture. And once we have it, we reduce government to the boring ass job that it really is and we try to get the ugliest, ugliest people to do this work. People that nobody should ever see in daylight need to be working in government because honestly, that's who they are on the inside right now. Let's get these people out of our lives. Let's push them to the boring administrative office. Let's remove their power by changing their data. But most importantly, let's deny giving them all of our attention. Let's tune out of the show so that ratings plummet and tune into each other so that we grow our culture back to what it truly is—the American story.

Divided, we fall, but united we stand. It is forever true, and we must unite. If you want to stand together and be empowered and control the way the nation goes, we have to be united despite our differences. It is the only way. And it takes a little bit of action each day from you and I and a little bit of deliberate, intentional ideological inconsistency to befuddle the system so its data is corrupted. Every time you reiterate something good, every time you reiterate something that is beneficial to us all, you do your part to change the culture. It is a small task that has a very big payoff. So stay focused, keep the faith and keep reiterating the plain truths right back into reality.

THE COURT OF
PUBLIC OPINION

Yes, there's chaos. Yes, there's madness. And yes, there's evil people in the world and some of them are our elected officials. One of the easiest and best ways to distract you is by creating an unbelievably evil bad guy narrative about an elected official in your mind and then creating a situation where you're led to believe that individual will be arrested and justice will be served. But if you're looking at the story with a long lens you'll notice that justice is never served, instead it's spread around like socialism to a few of the underlings associated with that individual, the associates who helped bring that individual to power. That's how justice is served. It's political revenge. And those who seek revenge should dig two graves, as the saying goes. That's why the subject has always changed right at the last minute. And how has the subject changed recently to continue the charade of bumping you along, hoping for the thing that will never happen and fighting against the thing that you can't prove happened—let me use an example that is going to piss some people off. Joe Biden's withdrawal from Afghanistan. Trump started the process and said, we have to get our troops out. That's exactly right. Trump took our party, the Republican Party, in a direction that was heading towards becoming more like the left—not in value, but in the tools and positions that we use to reach our goals. The culture being anti-war, being nationalist instead of globalist, those things were slowly changing but the first step, the big step, the thing Trump campaigned on was getting our troops home from Afghanistan. When Joe Biden executed that after "winning" the election, and (I do believe the election was rigged.) He executed it poorly. Or did he?

It's easy to sit back and say, *well, if Trump did it, it would have absolutely been better, it would have totally been spotless*, but you have to know that's unreasonable and that's not true. There is always things that happen that are unexpected. But the one thing that I really expected is that you would be bombarded with out of context information that would help draw you back to that moment of fighting for something that wasn't true. Fighting against something that probably didn't happen so that you could just waste more of your time. Exhibit A was the military dogs in cages images that went viral. The picture was lined up with cages that had service dogs in them, and it looked like they were cruely left behind and cold hearted Joe Biden was to blame. But the fact remains that could have been a picture of dogs that were being transported six or seven months ago from point A to point B. That could have been a picture of right before they were put on the airplane. None of that can be proven. But what can be proven is pundits on the right in their pursuit of distracting you from taking your eyes off the power (culture) and into the thing that is abstract, fooled you into getting really pissed off over a picture that was completely out of context after you have learned the hard way about out of context media over and over and over again because you defend Trump, rightly so, for the out of context videos and pictures used against him. You can't have it both ways and expect to ever win. You can't point out the game on one side and then when it's played against you, not see it. And if that is what happens to you, that means you're too emotional, easy to manipulate and you have to become more analytical. I agree with most everything that you probably agree with politically. I'm a pro-life, conservative Catholic. But I'm reasonable and I'm nuanced, and I understand that the real issue we have is not dogs being left behind in Afghanistan. Its monetized political pundits and the politicians using pundits to create narrative that's confusing, impossible to prove and ultimately an empty fight that draws you away from the target. The target is power. Power is attained through culture. And the culture in Washington that has been established is dividing the American people into camps. The two gulags. On the left they get what they ask for. On the right we get told what we want to hear. A man or woman is not guilty until they are proven guilty. Individuals must be viewed as innocent until that time. And that judgment rests on the provable existence of reasonable doubt. Reasonable doubt is the reason why our system upholds its justice in the proper way over time and reasonable doubt is what is being removed from the American mind and imagination. That is how political theatre works. One piece of evidence is cast down and a politicized story is built around it. And that story edifies all of the prejudices and the feelings and the understanding that the individuals have who are on the receiving end of it, perhaps they're naive about something, and the evidence then plays to them in a different way. Reasonable doubt is prudent. Reasonable doubt is something nobody wants you to have, because in politics, reality and power is created through story and then it is codified by removing reasonable doubt. And since all politics is narrative, you have to apply the courtroom filter to every bit of political news that you receive. Anything that you see, any story that is put before you in a political manner is one side of the story laying down evidence. The evidence is always tainted and it's always backed up by a story to make you believe the fake premise. Your job is to find the truth, to uncover the reasonable doubt and there's reasonable doubt that those dogs were left behind in a cage. There's reasonable doubt that the man dangling from the helicopter (another viral image of Biden abandoning people) was filmed exactly that week. There's reasonable doubt and almost everything that has been said about President Trump that you and I both know is not true. But reasonable doubt as a thought is removed from the conversation, removed from the possibility in your imagination because the storytelling is that powerful and can emotionally and psychologically press the right buttons so that you will never stop and calmly consider the evidence and search for reasonable doubt in order to maintain order and to reestablish peace among ourselves that will be reflected back to us in the media. We must value reasonable doubt as the thing that puts out all political fires and make these people prove their case instead of proving we are easy to manipulate. Don't let them get away with very simply jazzing up a scene, taking some evidence and planting it where they want it, finding it when they need it and using it in a story to make you forget that there is a potential, even the slightest bit of potential, that it is not true.

We the People are the court of public opinion. We're given tainted evidence all the time. As jurors sitting around who didn't ask to be locked down, who didn't ask to be told to stay home, who didn't want this globalist empire with China to be built by trade deals that our representatives made while working together to distract us, both left and right, by fighting over inflated versions of good guys and bad guys and by worrying about the simplest stupidest things that are no skin off anyone's back—we must reverse it and start embracing our role as the jurors. The news and the politicians are all competing lawyers that work for different clients, and those clients have stories that they're trying to manipulate. One way or another each piece of evidence that is put in front of us must be scrutinized. And if you can find any reasonable doubt whatsoever, you have to dismiss the story as false and irrelevant to your life. There's too much at stake. It's our freedom that is at stake. This isn't a game of right versus left, or *they got him this time but we'll get them next time.* There is no next time. It's been completely exposed and it's obvious to anybody looking with an honest set of eyes. There's one party in the United States of America, and it is called the Government, and the government operates both political identities and uses them as their lawyers, who then present evidence to the American people that is tainted and false. Reasonable doubt shuts down their game. Make them make their case before you get so aggravated that you will let them steal another year of our lives because there is a schedule that the media goes on that is concocted with the government and the schedule is not yours. Resist being distracted away from the target itself, which is power and know that power comes from culture and culture is gained by us creating it by, We the People, not They/Them the corporations and the officials that they paid for. We've got to change this game and I feel that the time has come. Everybody sees it and everybody knows it. So put on your juror outfit and pay attention to the evidence because nine times out of ten, there's so much reasonable doubt that you have to let it go. With your help and a little bit of closer attention paid to the mechanics of political narrative, we can overcome the division done to us by storytelling. We tell our own stories and we tell them to each other and we embrace each other's unique journey through the United States of America, and we will be halfway home to getting over this awful period in American history.

THE MAULING OF
AMERICANS

I n 1956, communist leader Nikita Khrushchev said *we will take America without firing a shot. We do not have to invade the United States. We will destroy you from within.* Does that sound like something that is unfolding right now in your daily life? It's because it is. It's because storytelling, divisive storytelling, false narratives, personalities that point you to chaos and destruction nonstop are all helping achieve this goal of destroying us from within. And we have the power to stop it because the battlefield is in our own country. It's our daily life. It's the things we do to make America, America. And if the thing that we spend most of our time doing is reacting to false stories that are meant to destroy us from within, well, we deserve what we get. But if we wise up and we realize that we have each other, we have freedom, and for the most part Americans really could give two shits about what people do in their personal lives—if we can stop this abuse of media and narrative that is only meant to divide Americans, only meant to keep us pitted against one another and balkanized in our little bitter groups, if we can stop that, we put an end to this. We can put an end to being destroyed from within. We can put an end to this whole entire game, which is tearing our country apart and doesn't have to. It's up to us. It truly, truly is up to us, the citizens of the United States, not our political leaders, not our television personalities, not our monetized Pundicrats, not our cable news personalities. None of it. What the left has figured out and the left really does stand for communism when it comes to a global left, a global left is not the people that you think of fondly as the artistic left wingers of the 1960s who were trying to change the conversation about the way that American life was lived and bringing different representation to people who, be honest, were really left out of the conversation back then. But that created an opening for the Communists to come in and manipulate. And one of the greatest ways that this manipulation happened is Communists figured out how to show American leaders in media and in government how to make Communism profitable and enjoyable for themselves. It's not enjoyable to you and I. But it is enjoyable to our elites, to our people who are on the receiving end of massive payments from foreign nations that are meant to destroy America from within. That is the attack. We go out into this world where we think that we're the badass country that tells everybody how they're going to live their life with our pop culture. And then our pop culture is seeded with foreign money that foreign money tells the folks who are involved in pop culture that they have to make entertainment that appeals to a wider audience, a globalist audience. Well, you do realize that America won the Cold War because the audience in the world was drawn to our story of Liberty. So what are we drawing the audience to now? A story that America is not relevant anymore, that America's liberty is a thing of the past, that the computer age, the technology age, the age of everything being run by algorithms that can be made to steer society in any direction that the programmers choose. The world they want us to live in is going to permanently put an end to the

American way if we don't collectively say no and push back.

You'll find that there's a lot of people on the Pundicrat right who are always advocating for a second economy. These people want a divided America. Their argument is that Big Tech has banned conservative speech that Big Tech has banned things that conservatives like and we can't exist, and therefore we need a second economy. That's the enemy's agenda! The enemy would like to break America in half and have a dual existence that eliminates our global power permanently. We can't go there. We cannot go to this situation where we say, *Oh well, the globalists and the communists they won. Therefore, let's divide America up and have our own little secret club over here where we've monetized everything and we get you guys to dance around and buy our merch in this new second economy. We've got to have credit cards for conservatives. We need websites for conservatives. We need all these different things...for conservatives.* No. We don't. What we need to do as conservatives is reach across the aisle and embrace our liberal brothers and sisters who are American born Americans or naturalized citizens. And we need to form a unified front and push back against this ridiculous attempt to divide the United States of America into two economies. Nobody should want this. Instead we ought to change the culture. We don't want to be attacked by the media anymore. The road to this goal is about a 10 to 20 year journey of not being distracted off the mission of not being manipulated into falling for charlatans, into not putting all your eggs in the basket of any political candidate or party. But instead you should start practicing unpredictable ideological inconsistency. Being American on the Fourth of July weekend is easy. You live and you let live. People who have a big party in their backyard and they happen to be a gay family, and they have all kinds of stuff going on that the folks maybe two blocks away would never have in their backyard is to be ignored because the American way is live and let live. We still need some common ground, some common space where we all agree on the rule of law and the way our system and our society is going to be broadcast out to the public for the health of the public. And so the communists and the globalists have really identified this little intersection of civic life in the United States as the place to really tear us apart but they're doing it with smoke and mirrors. They're doing it with the same trick that Hollywood has always used to establish its celebrities, it's legends, myths, everything delivered in little bits of information that don't make a lot of sense until pieced together and spoon fed to you by storytellers across a symphonic reiteration that makes it make sense in your mind.

We have to to be symphonic reiterators of truth. That's why we must escape the storytelling system's lies and not let it follow us because it can't follow us to where we need to go. The manipulation can't follow you offline. Localism exists offline. All this online manipulation and desire to keep you spinning your tires in mud, never progressing but always fighting over the fake things, always fighting over the things that are intentionally made outrageous so that you will be distracted by them, this is nothing more than the mauling of Americans by the Communist Bear, and the bear is a mirage, a digital mirage, a storytelling device that attacks us on the regular. But we have to walk into the attack while also disengaging with the lies. We have to participate in the battle of nonsense on some levels. The nonsense battle is going to get turned up very soon, and this is going to be a very important time for us as a people who are divided going into some critical elections. Right now it feels like the Left and the Communists have achieved their goal of completely destroying the town square in our minds. The general space that we all share in our is polluted with communist storytelling, division, outrage and violence and all the things that, the more you look at them, the more they become a horrifying reality in your imagination. But we, as free people, have a chance going into the 2024 Presidential election to surprise and shock the world by being Americans again, not by participating and celebrating the destruction of the democrats or the destruction of the republicans, or why Joe Biden shits his pants and wears diapers, or why Trump is the rightful president. We have to back away from all that theater of the absurd. Yeah, the 2020 election was rigged or stolen. I'm never going to disagree with that. I saw it with my own eyes. I live in Pennsylvania and personally know people who dropped off ballots in drop boxes and they weren't counted, and those people contacted our state senators. And it went on in all these different states too but I'm not going to even bother with that because we have to live life going forward. We have to think forward, we have to think strategically and also as a group of people, as Americans who are divided, our very first step has to be to purposefully unite. Every time a political party sweeps into power and the other one loses, there's commercials you see that are advertising the United States as a place where united we stand divided we fall. And the side that's on the losing end, the people that are on the bitter losing end that are really dialed into the slanted political story, they always probably have this internal conversation with themselves. *Yeah, well, we wouldn't be so divided if it wasn't for the other side.* And that goes both ways. To unite as Americans going forward and into the next election we must put an end to the ridiculous divisions that we are all being exhausted by and it is going to require rising above politics as citizens. It doesn't mean that politics aren't going to happen. Politics is a part of life and the truest statement is all politics are local. So on this collective national stage on this theatrical show that we all tune into and participate in, it's time to say to each other that leaders on both sides of the aisle, leaders and corporations have taken the power of the United States Constitution away from the people. It's manipulated. It's used for dividing Americans instead of empowering the people, so it's up to us to rise above all of it. Take a look from a very wide angle view at the playing field and the personalities that haven't changed and the payments that have gone out and the bribes that have happened. We have to just rise above it and say, *Listen, if you're one of the groups of people that have grievances that the news media is using to divide Americans at this point in time, it's going to be someone else later. You have to step back for the greater good and say enough enough dividing.* And if the media doesn't want to respond to that, if our government officials don't like the sound of uniting, they'll show you by trying to make us go even more bizarre and crazy at each other's throats. So it's a secret war that we're in, it's a whisper campaign. It's *yeah, I'm a Republican, but I really am an American or I'm a Democrat, but ultimately I'm an American citizen.* We have to reclaim and retake what is ours. This land is our land. It truly is. And if you're blessed enough to be born here and if you're blessed enough to have been granted citizenship here, guess what time it is—it's time to look after the store because it's being robbed by Globalists and Communists and there's nothing they'd like to do more than to divide the store in two so that the customer is never right, but he can just go shop on the other side if he doesn't like what he sees here. That's not the United States of America and that's not celebrating all of our differences. That's not embracing all the diversity that we have in this country that comes to us in the form of food and artwork, cultural stories, legends, things that we share, things that are all added to the melting pot and come out as the American story in all of its diversity. You can't have that when you have an evenly divided nation that is really monetized so that elites in power can stay elites in power, choose their replacements and maintain an un-free world that is run by systems and computers and a hand picked select group of human beings who decide the fate of the rest of us. I don't know about you, but that's not the future I want, and I doubt that's the future that any human being wants who walks the face of this Earth. People want to be free. People want to explore. People want to express themselves. And some people want to just live simply and not be bothered. All of those options are available in American life and they're plentiful. Amish communities live up the street from me in rural Pennsylvania where it becomes farmland, Amish farms and people who are living very far removed from some of the realities that you and I live with. But they're just a few miles down the road from me. And that's the United States. I can take another turn and go about 10 or 15 more miles and find hipster cafes and marijuana stores. This is America. America should have this diversity reflected in the landscape of its people. What it shouldn't have is a (staged) bitterly divided political class that maintains the divisions among people to maintain their power. Celebrate your independence. Celebrate the idea in your mind that just a hop, skip and a jump from you is a totally different world and a totally different group of people—but they're all Americans and as Americans we have our greatest gifts which is our freedom and our Liberty. We must defend our freedom and Liberty at all costs and that means if both political parties are corrupt and if both political parties have ruined the way that we think about them, if they have ruined their reputations, we punish them by ignoring them and removing all of their power.

REAL REPUBLICANS

I hope that you take advantage of your freedom and you get together with your family and you spend time together appreciating the things that make our country great, starting with the freedom to move about and live your life as you choose, because there really is no greater freedom than that being free to move about and live your life as you wish. I'm somebody who's lived in multiple states. I left a small town and I moved to New York City. I went from New York City to Los Angeles. I went from Los Angeles to New Jersey. I went from New Jersey to Pennsylvania. I've moved about and lived my life as I needed or as I wanted to in my own pursuit of happiness. And that very essential basic freedom that we are all born with when we're born in the United States of America is really what's at stake if we allow the government to keep playing this charade like we have two sides. I want you to reflect on something over the holiday season, a pattern that I've seen emerge in the narrative of the Republican Party over the last 25 years. It's very strange to me, but everybody who rises to power in the Republican Party is a self-proclaimed ex liberal and they use this storyline that, *I finally am seeing clearly and I have woken up. I've got it right in my head and I used to be fooled by the other side, but now I'm moving into this side.* That's how we get Donald Trump as President. He's a self-proclaimed ex-liberal. We get commentators who have the most followers and the biggest impact on where the the narrative of the right goes. Ex liberals, all of them, self-proclaimed. The reason for this is painfully obvious. Liberals run the show. They are the ones who use and abuse this hollowed out fake version of Abraham Lincoln's Republican Party, which became Ronald Reagan's Republican Party. They used it as a hand puppet to generate all the outrage they need for the much larger audience they've cultivated through mainstream media. If we ever really did get a Republican president, he would never act like the ones who have been elected that have pretended to be Republican presidents. Sure, there's been some great legislation that came from Trump or even George W. Bush but Bush went around growing the government, creating agencies that didn't exist before the left provided fake outrage that passionately made us support him. It's a very clear, deceptive game of divide the people, not just to conquer them, but to consolidate power. I want to know where the real Republicans are? I actually know the answer to that question. The real Republicans are normal people who have a decent common sense about them, recognizing that the government should never be so big that it has the power to infiltrate every detail of your life. Real Republicans are everywhere except in power. They're represented by disingenuous echoes of what they believe. So why do we keep getting the coastal elites to represent us? We need a Republican from the middle of nowhere. We need a real Republican because a real Republican would address the problems much differently than a hand puppet of the left.

There was a popular news segment program in 1980s called On the Road, hosted by Charles Kuralt and it aired on CBS. It was a time when a reporter being a journalist had the curiosity to go past the chaos and into the lives of everyday Americans to discover that the chaos does not exist within them, but instead only on the shows that we put on television, only on the news that we get collective anxiety over. Only on the business model that is destroying all unity now, which didn't have the power then that it does now thanks to technology which automates systems. The American people exist outside of the circles of influence and far away from the exclusive small stage concocted by the left so they can force you to look at life through out of context information about your country and about the people who live in it. Outside of that fake frame still exists the interesting, talented, amazing, capable, beautiful, free American people, but corporate culture is used to define the political reality, and the culture does not reflect the character of the real people of the United States because the real character of the United States is very similar to the character of a real human being, someone with a complex past but who is constantly improving and changing and learning from their experiences and lessons. Someone with a complex nature, kindness always available and sternness when needed. The American people are mostly alike and nothing like the news portrays us. Keep that in mind as you celebrate the holidays and you look around at the family members you disagree with. Your fellow countrymen who you are made to believe are very far apart from what you value is make believe because we're all Americans. We all live under the same blessed situation, and we cannot let that situation be altered or perverted or changed because we have an addiction to political news and political storytelling that makes us forget who we really are. This is a very big uphill battle that requires patience and focus. And as a true grassroots movement, I ask nothing of you other than you adopt this mindset and reiterate the true things because reiteration makes the nation. And now together, we can create a new sub pop culture that will usher in a new political reality. May God continue bless America.

A TRAGEDY OF
SHARERS

I n the world of media, the world of spin, the world
of opportunities to become rich, famous and then
richer and infamous, exist in multitudes like never
before. There are so many outlets, so many ways to express yourself and monetize it. So ask yourself—why do
so many choose to express themselves purely on the
stage of partisan politics? What is it about politics that
draws people to use whatever vocation and talent they
have to exploit the political trivialities just to further
their personal brands? I think it's a pretty obvious answer when you step back and look at it—everybody in
America wants to be famous one way or another. Being
a celebrity in America makes you American Royalty and
the public is encouraged to seek it by a pop culture marketplace that depends on it. There was a time when
fame was tied to circumstance, meaning the circum-
stances of someone's organic rise to notoriety made
them well known and therefore, famous. The best way
to become famous is not to try, but just do great work in
life. Do the things that you love, and if enough people
recognize it and celebrate it as a group, that's a wonderful win. Actors used to enjoy this success because audiences would respond to the performances and say, *you
know the character that you played, you played it so well,*

really touched me, really moved me, and that interaction, that celebration of the artist's craft as an actor or the writer's craft as the screenwriter or the director, was all about the art itself. Whereas now the craft has turned into a device for corporate advertising and political theater. It's a sad situation we're in because influencers, if you think about it, are an invention of the corporate world. The corporate world pays political influencers to sell lifestyle and ideologies that help sell more corporate products. So if you're playing this game as a political pundit, you become a mini Avon salesmen for viagra, lifetime supplies of canned food and gold bullion that you'll need when the apocalypse strikes. The result of this two decade long cycle of the right not having a voice in culture has resulted art that has no value because it's completely one sided and political, leaving no value to any of the things that used to be wonderful because we enjoyed them for what they were. A group of people who make a movie and just tell a story, for example. And in that story is a character that struggles and when that character overcomes the struggle is something to celebrate and something to be impressed by. You really showed the human struggle in a dramatic way, and that story uplifted and changed my perception a little. Made me think. But because the left discovered that their power is tied to using storylines to change the way people think *politically* and because it's proven successful over and over again, it has created an unlimited supply of rats who come running out of the gutters, looking for their chance to get up and tap dance politics in front of you their way. It's kind of like a contest to see who can be the best tap dancer for the main stream media. So if you look at it the way I do, you'll start to see the comedy in the show. You'll start to see that a fake story is blown out of proportion, and then you can hysterically watch everybody run to it and pour gas on it. Let's not get mad about this parlor trick anymore. Let's start mocking it. Mocking the Devil is how you make him go away. The Devil can't stand to be mocked, so mock, ridicule pick on and never stop giving the suspicious eye to people who are selling political theater to you. We have to end this cottage industry that is blown way out of proportion.

When I started out in show business a long time ago, there wasn't as many people involved in it as there is today. Let me explain what I mean. There was a time when it was a very hard bubble to penetrate and to get in required a full commitment a really good that got you noticed and there was lots of competition and it was merit based. Now, because the audience has been so cleverly divided into different subgroups and markets, that is really how this new business model happened where talent is secondary to the message. So the message is what's more important. People are out there like clowns trying to show that they can divide the public better than the other guy on the inside. That's the accounting that's taking place *we've secured this much of the audience, they get that much of the audience. Let's draw them over here. Let's keep these people here. Let's sell these guys this stuff.* That's really the the accounting that they do. At the end of the day, they're not thinking *I went out and told the truth and because I told the truth, the world is after me so please donate.* I'm telling you the full truth right now. It's all a big game. All of it. None of it matters. You have to understand that if you want to play the game, go ahead and play it, but don't get emotionally drawn into it and think that it's anything other than a power game because story involves an emotional reaction, so the pros always try to get an emotional reaction out of you so that you'll stay married to their storyline.

I am a Republican and I have been a Republican my entire life. As soon as I turned old enough to register with selective services I went to the post office in my town and signed up and I chose the Republican Party because Ronald Reagan was the president and I loved Ronald Reagan, and I love my country and I love my flag. But I don't need to go out and prove that to you, and I don't need you to prove that to me so that we can establish a gulag where we're like, *Hey, we're the ones who love America, and you don't,* because that's bullshit and you know it. You want to know who loves America? Somebody who gets up and builds their business. Somebody who gets up and takes care of their family. Somebody who moves the ball forward locally in their own community, that's loving America. People who get glued to political stories are tearing apart America. And it only benefits our government, which wants to get bigger and bigger and bigger and bigger. It's at the point where it's about to swallow us all whole. So here we are, we're in the belly of the whale and we've got distractions everywhere when what we need to do is work together and get a big giant staff and prop that whale's mouth open so it can't close, then run out of it as fast as possible and swim away and let it sink to the bottom of the ocean. Because it's a fake dead whale, it's blubber is just blubber. There's nothing to it. It's not good for you and it's not good for me. It belongs in the depths of the ocean where nobody can hear it, where nobody can see it. And when the people are free from the scam and the con of modern politics, what do you think happens? What do you think is the result of this large group of people that are all like minded and working together to divide us left and right? What do you think happens? I'll tell you— they will start to panic. That's right. The same thing that Pundicrats say about their targets all the time, which is always fake. *They're panicking!* Now these guys are going to panic. The whole organization of people who are benefiting from our mindless divisions will panic. Not only will they panic, but they won't have the mousetrap working for themselves anymore, and they'll have to go and reinvent their wheel. And we have to know that they're going to try and reinvent the wheel, and we've got to keep flattening it every time until these people come to heel qnd promote things that are truly going to be good for American culture and society. I really want nothing to do with this right wing narrative anymore. It doesn't represent the Republican Party or represent me. I would vote for Donald Trump if he came back and survived the primaries, because of the policies. It's the policies that matter, but it's the presentation of them that wins or loses or unites or keeps us divided. And the political narrative guys are all about keeping us divided because they've carved out a very sizable chunk of an audience that if it just married itself to the other side temporarily, would unite in a way that would end the entire Conservatism Inc. game. You know Biden goes around saying we've got to unite, but he doesn't really push it because the government doesn't want the people united. A united people is the end of the tyranny of division. A united people is the end of anti-Americanism that is fueled by globalists who are paying our politicians and our pundits and anybody that can be influencers secretly for globalism by keeping Americans pitted against one another. They achieve their goals over and over again because we allow it, so join me and reject this. Reject this presentation of division. Reject seeing the same video over and over again of police officers getting attacked by citizens that can give a crap about law and order. Don't let them lead you by the nose to bonfires of insanity every day, while one of them goes on the other side and pours gas on it while the other points and says, *Look at that thing, it's coming for you next.* No, it's not. There's people that live in cities that are really intensely close to some bitter divisions in society. But it's not as widespread as storytelling makes you believe. Making you believe chaos is unstoppable makes you a customer for life. These personalities on the right, if they had to, they would go and punch themselves in the face on stage and say, *Can you believe that guy hit me?* And then they would mount an entire social media campaign against their right hand by taking every bad moment and magnifying it, turning it into a business model. I've got a real beef with guys who grift and take this party and the people in it and manipulate them for their own gain. I think it's disgusting. It's what the left does, which is why I call them Pundicrats.

The margin of unity in this country is razor thin. It's not like we're so divided that it's impossible to put back together. That's why media goes batshit crazy all the time, getting you to go batshit crazy with them so that you don't realize it's just takes a few people moving this way or that way and then it's over for them. I want to see that day. I want to see this politics only fire that these guys start get put out. I want to see the people that they thought were tuned in to the bonfire of insanity, to surprise them and suddenly show up with buckets of water poured on the fire. Let these guys choke on the smoke of their lies. The whittling away of American power is nothing more than a tragedy of sharers. Stop sharing anything that divides Americans. Stop participating in the tragedy and start putting your effort where you know it belongs right in front of your face with what you're working on. Your day. Your community, your local world. The people you can influence may be as small as opening the door for somebody, but you're not selling a corporate product, you're restoring unity through your influence and kindness. You're restoring the American way, which is live and let live. Enjoy your freedom and enjoy the gifts that have been given to you and always work to move these fake hustlers off the stage and enjoy all the opportunity that they've sucked up for 30 to 40 years so that you can't really have it. It's time to take it back. No more tragedy of sharers. The American dream is back and it's a dream of opportunity, liberty and justice for all.

CREATE FUN

The new symphonic reiteration of reality is beginning to make progress changing the narrative so that it is telling a story about We the People and the true things that matter to us that also keep us united and powerful over the system. But maintaining that story depends on a culture, and that culture depends on you and me. This chapter is about the joyful creation of fun, how creating is fun, how spending your time away from the madness, away from the insanity, away from the lies, enables you to re-experience life almost like an innocent child. That's why so many people who are artists that create and spend their time in the arts appear to be young at heart and young at mind, and not to be taken seriously by folks who demand seriousness from everybody at all times. But the artist's ability to create culture is extremely powerful, so powerful that for the majority of artists, they really have no idea what they're doing to contribute to a culture that is removing liberty little by little from the American people. They just know that they want to create. They just know that they're good at this one thing and it brings them joy to do it for others. Somebody can write a story, somebody can paint a painting, somebody can can write a song—but in order to increase the likeliness that it will be successful there exists too many options for them to back into the political needs of the already established corporate culture, which has been corporatized against liberty and the American way, because that's the market has been created. The 1960s artists movement, the movement that wanted to break away from the system and the man has become the system and the man, and that is to be expected and anticipated of our movement too when sub pop culture is successful, it will become corporatized because the resistance will have disappeared. The ability to say no will go away because we will overwhelm the system, and it will seem reasonable that NBC wants to have some creator who came up through the sub pop cult movement to have their show on TV. It will seem like we wiped away the past and we're now in a better future and it's all the same game and the left knows this potential scenario as well. That's why they're in the mode they're in at this current moment—to stall or prevent anyone from knocking them off the game board, but we're going to do that because we figured out the right way. It's not to attack from the top. It's to come up from the bottom. And that means creating art and culture in any way possible. But it also means doing it with a very specific purpose in mind, and that is restoration Americana. That doesn't mean you're only making art and stories and things that reflect the. American Revolution. That's part of history that must be celebrated and known and appreciated, but to get to the to the general public, to get to the people who are the majority of the people too busy living life and caught in between competing messages. Normies are always falling on the left hand side because ultimately they use every tool at their disposal to create an insane version of a Republican so that no large ground of people can see eye to eye with them. That means your art has to be in line with modern life as its starting point and from there you can go anywhere. That doesn't mean that it doesn't have

God embedded into its meaning either. It means that you, as an artist, have to really think of yourself as a fisherman and your art is the hook. And on that hook is various things that you've created. And when you catch somebody with that hook and you slowly reel them in, they don't know where they're being pulled but you're pulling them closer to the truth through your art. A lot of people strongly know the truth and want to slam it in front of your face until you accept it or not. But there's no empathy there. There's no understanding that everybody's on their own journey and not everybody is on the same page at the same time. And this reluctance, this pride, this inability to go down to the small space and talk among ourselves, that's what holds us back from winning any cultural influence. Pride is killing the right, and that's why the left is always increasing false pride over the wrong things. What I want us to be proud of is that we got everybody saying the same thing, that we got everyone wearing a style according to what we think is best, that We the People take control of the narrative instead of They the government and Them the corporations. That's the real they/them that we're up against. It's not trans people that you run into that are working at a store and you ask somebody for help and it's a person who turns around that looks like the Joker. That's not your enemy, believe it or not, that's a very insignificant small number of people, put right in front of you politically. It's a perfect distraction, and it makes you go, *What is going on here?* When really, you should just ignore it, laugh at it and say, *That's what the left did with their cultural power? They ran out of ideas so they just went for insanity because insanity stops the game clock.* We have to create fun because fun is what gets it going again and the left is good at creating fun as well because they have so many of the levers of cultural power under their control so they can distract you in one space and then they can entertain you in the next space. That's how much power the left has. They put out a group of people dancing over the coronavirus and for those of us tuned in to the political right hand side of things, we say *this is so stupid the world is on fire, everything is going wrong, freedom is being torn away, would you look at these people dancing and performing a song about how much they love the vaccine.* But there's a trick going on there, that lighthearted fun show that some people catch in a few minutes registers in their mind as: Democrats equal fun, lighthearted, something that's not threatening while the right paints a picture of itself as: demanding, overbearing, schooling everybody that they're wrong. If we become artist fishermen, we can change that dynamic to our advantage.

Creating fun art, fun stories, fun things that hit the culture points shouldn't be looked at by any Christian who listens to my podcast or is reading this book as against God. That's false and also how the left so easily attacks religion. Joy is part of Christian life but many people will dial that down to *my only joy is when I'm with Jesus, or my only joy is when I'm sitting in church praying.* That is not true. That's not representative of the human experience, human nature as it was designed by God is full of unique expressions of humanity. You can dance to any song you want. You can watch movies. You can read stories about crazy human beings doing crazy inhuman things. You can listen to songs that tell the weirdest story about disconnect from love or obsession with another human being. All of those things exist, and you can enjoy them for what they are. But guess what? You can create them as well. You can create better versions of pop culture and can fish and lead people into a fun dance song, but the hidden message is something that has to do with where you want to draw the culture, which is back to a place of reasonability, back to a place of unity, back to an understanding that it's not left versus right. It's not gay versus straight. It's not this versus that. It's We the People versus government power. Right now the people are scattered, scrambled, confused while the government is unified around one message pretending to fight each other on our behalf. They pretend so if we the game, we have to stop bitterly fighting each other and start pretending to fight each other, but have a secret language, a secret understanding that it's really just to distract the government from its own momentum. What we really ought to spend our time and energy on is dialing down their story and becoming the authors of the new story of what it means to be an American citizen, an American individual person in the year 2023 and beyond. The audience is crying out for fresh art and a new way to engage, and the left doesn't have the answer because what people really want is their liberty back, their privacy back. They want unity back, but are easily distracted away from that power. And the people who can change it the most are the folks who are on the outs, the people on the right. And so we're the most distracted of them all. So don't be distracted. Wake up with intent the same way you do about taking care of your diet or your exercise or your way of life, know that you owe the culture one little nudge per day, per week, per month, that you can contribute. Restoration Americana depends on millions and millions of small, constant expressions of the positive truth that we want to bring into reality. By millions and millions of small reiterations of the true things, we will start to change the entire conversation. So look at politics for what it really is. It's an industry that is preventing the people from having power. It wasn't supposed to be that way. It was supposed to be how we negotiated things, how we went back and forth, how we engaged the big problems and came to solutions, but it's ruined by the other side intentionally so that it doesn't work anymore. There is nothing we can do with it. But culture is impossible to ruin. They can take it and make it out of reach, which is what they've tried to do, but we are going to embrace our smallness and we're going to reach to each other and form this new symphonic reiteration of through small pieces of art.

I want to tell you a little bit about my writing process because I think it has something to do with the greater experience that an artist has and is close to some truth for a lot of people that try to create. Creating is arranging and organizing things into a palpable expression. It's about taking chaos and organizing it into something artistic that says something to other people. So as a writer, I feel like the the thing about writing is you're taking a big idea and you're arranging it dramatically. It's no different than arranging physical objects. I can't get into doing much creative work unless I have the physical world around me arranged in a way that is conducive to my productivity. Some people can have a big mess all around them, and that's how they get to their moment of creativity. Everybody is different, but the organizing of an idea, synthesizing it into something that is an artistic expression that metaphorically tells the truth about the bigger picture is what we're looking for here. We're not looking for people who, you know, have mastered hitting the nail on the head. We're looking for those subversive things, those subversive moments that reel the person closer to the truth. If I had to identify the most important thing we can do, it's maintaining an indie culture (that I participate in) because I know how the culture at the top end works. Intellectual property creation through storytelling is vital to growing a new culture. If you have it in you to write a novel, to write a story and you can make it seem like it's about some people pulling off a bank heist, but really, what it's about is some saving grace between two humans that reconnects them to something beautiful and outside of human reality, you've got to go for it, you've got to try and do it, whatever the story is. If you're an artist and a graphic designer, graphic design things that reiterate the message that it's the culture that matters. There's a very famous saying from James Carville when he was running the Clinton campaigns. He came up with the phrase, *It's the economy stupid*, and that was to tell everyone in politics, *Hey, hey, hey, there's only one thing that matters. And it's the economy.* And he was right. And it was a very potent message. So I've turned that into our own very potent message for sub pop cult, which is *it's the culture stupid*. And that should be your answer to anyone who tries to make it all politics all the time. *It's the culture stupid.* Make that into a saying and popularize it. Put it in your art. Spray paint it on walls, whatever you have to do. Look at how the left handled the 1960s to get themselves in power today and do the same exact thing but put your message in it, put your heart in it, put your understanding of the truths in it because I tell you this as a fact, if enough people reiterate it, you won't even hear the side that makes you angry or turns you off anymore because there's too many of us, we have the potential to be overwhelmingly loud. And the only way to prevent our powerful voice is by scattering us to the wind with false narratives and false hopes. Falsely chasing after justice that never comes. False storylines, false understandings of the true dynamics of power and how it works, all of that prevents this one critical thing that we need to do. So spend your time a little better, spend your time creating, look at the news and say, *you know, that's never going to be anything other than a dumpster fire* and stop watching dumpster fires for the rest of your life. You see it. You know what it is, you have it categorized, it's never going to change. Don't let them fool you ever again. Undo the left's power with something artistic, even if it's in your own mind and your own world, and it's only seen by a select group of people in your own social network following, it has impact. You have to understand that it has significant impact. A little bit of unity, a little bit of coming to the center, a little bit of drawing people closer together is like kryptonite to the mess that they put upon us. So everybody should produce art and hurt the left where they will really hurt, the place that they run unopposed —the culture.

LET US ENTERTAIN
YOU

Always stay focused on the mission at hand, the all important mission of raising up an independent sub pop culture in the United States that can replace and supersede the corporate culture that poisons everything it touches. I know you can feel it because I can feel it. The winds of change are blowing. Some people say the paradigm has shifted or is shifting. I don't believe that, but I do believe that everything does have a season and the season of political narrative being used to destroy all unity in Americans and simply create more consumers who are better at consuming and therefore get consumed, is over. We're on to the next chapter and in the next chapter there is nothing more interesting than independent American artists creating their own content and making a modest living. The creator economy, the influencer economy, those two blend together, but they're not the same thing. Creators provide art, context, meaning—something that is fulfilling and satisfying to your soul that is searching for beauty seen in someone else's interpretation of the life, the world, their experiences. And everyone's experience is different, but all bound together by one unique, incredible quality that is the freedom of being an American citizen. I have friends who are filmmakers that were born and raised on Indian reservations and make movies about that experience. I have friends who are born into wealth on the Upper East side of New York City, and they tell stories about that experience. The problem is the people with the wealth and the connectivity have consolidated the access points, consolidated the narrative itself so that it's mainly populated and controlled by people of means. They try to cover for this by selecting one group of people and pretending to liberate them but everyone knows it's an act. There's a lots of talent in this country. It is overflowing in fact, but it's constantly caught in these political honey traps, which diminish the ability for us to collectively get on board with celebrating who we really are. We really truly are free Americans. That means the freedom of one person to live the completely opposite of you has to be something that you cherish as a feature, not a bug. The thing that the politicians do and their pundits and the folks that are always preventing us from getting to the moment of unity, what they always try to focus you on is how the other person's expression of freedom is somehow impacting your life but nine times out of ten that's not true and you know it. It's only true in the public square. But these examples that are used to keep us agitated and divided are on very thin grounds. You take a look at the whole nation and you can say to yourself, *a certain number of people are going to die in a car accident today,* but you don't ever see the news constantly going over each individual car accident to make it seem like everybody's crashing into everybody else. But that's what they do. That's what they do with political narrative. And again, it's to prevent this moment of truth from happening. It's to prevent this beautiful thing that can occur when we really all officially turn away from the corporate media. And you have to understand something, corporate media means corporate media and corporate interests means profits. Profits mean repeat customers because repeat customers mean the corporate narrative is working.

Look at all of the dreams you've had and the things that you've wanted to do as seeds that you're trying to grow and you plant the seed and you prepare the dirt and you get it started and then what happens? A storm comes along, a torrential rain shower, an unexpected flood that washes away the garden bed and forces you to have to start again. That's really what the news does and what the political narrative hucksters do to all of your dreams. They keep telling you that the garden bed is actually not ready, that you're going to have to do a whole bunch of work and start all over. So why bother? But that's the opposite of what will happen if you push through. What I do here with sub pop cult is a little bit like a river. It's flowing from my podcast and this book out into the world. I'm not trying to flood the world. I'm trying to erode the corporate narrative very slowly, and over time, it'll happen. You've seen the Grand Canyon. That didn't happen overnight, and just getting this ball rolling is really what it takes. But you picking it up and carrying it the rest of the way and passing it to the next person is also what it takes, because that's what they do on the corporate media side. They play pass the baton among themselves. So we have one giant story wall, one loud, obnoxious wall of storytelling that is pre-selected only using the things that will piss people off and keep them staring at that big giant wall. But if we turn around and we do little plays for each other and we start watching folk films, we start buying indie art and we start searching for independent authors—if we do that en masse, what good is that wall anymore? What good is that distraction? That thing that they want us to stare at that only they hold the projectors for? This is what I'm trying to get you to understand, and very slowly, you're going to see that I'm accurate in my observations and I'm true in my ask. I'm only asking you to do one thing—either create independent art or become a patron of independent art. You don't need all those subscriptions. Keep Netflix, keep whatever one you want, but you don't need 50 million things. What you do need is that one really good independent film about somebody's struggle in life that uplifts you, uplifts your family, makes people feel good again. You need that great story written by an unknown author in the middle of nowhere that tells the truth about justice in the United States. You don't need a gaslit political narrative to tell you what is good and what isn't and what's worth your time, because most of the things you're gaslit into paying attention to are about draining your time and making you impotent when it comes to creativity and making you a reactionary instead of a revolutionary. Aren't you bored of this game that they keep playing? Decade after decade passing the baton within a small circle that gets smaller and smaller and smaller? I am. I'm tired of it. I'm desperate for somebody to go out there and make a great piece of work that we can all rally behind and say, amen, this is what it's all about. This is the best story. Once we do that, that wall has a giant crack in it and that day is coming, my friends. I don't know who's going to deliver that wrecking ball, but it's coming. And the glorious era, the future that we all can bring about really does require the collective turning away from what you know to be false. I'm not saying don't enjoy your freedom and do all the things that you like to do in this great, wonderful land of ours. I'm saying recognize that the class warfare, the race warfare, every division that is monetized and called warfare is false. There's only one warfare and it's the corporations taking over and manipulating the freedom of the people. Corporations consolidate power. They handpick people to continue us down this path of slowly acting like a toxic river that erodes freedom. Join my river and start to erode their entire narrative because it's poison. It is meant to kill freedom. It is meant to kill individual liberty. It is meant to empower those already in power. That's not the way our country was designed to work, and it's only happened because the human spirit has a design flaw itself. It has a weakness for power and gold and shiny things, and everybody is corruptible, myself included—everyone. The resistance that I'm seeking from you is a resistance that is the hardest resistance of them all. Resist the world, resist all of its lies, resist all of its invitations to waste your precious time, the seasons of your life. Don't waste it propping up politics. With your help we are going to turn this culture around and make it answer to the people, the free people of the United States of America, not the creations of corporations who then feed back into Democrats who then consolidate power. It's time, my friends, I've seen enough and you've seen enough. Let's move forward together with one same goal of overturning the corporate narrative so the story is about you and I and not about they and them.

BUILD LITTLE
BRIDGES

Winter is here, and it's not the winter that the left expected, it's the winter that they cultivated by installing Joe Biden as president of the United States. The revelation that is clear to all of us is that the government is not run by those we elect. Instead, it is run by a symphony of like minded people who have their tentacles in both sides of the political divide. The left and the right are both corporate iterations of the federal government, and they are used to keep us divided and separate from each other. They are used to inflate one side and pit it against the other. I will say this often because it is quickly forgotten. The left is diabolical. It knows how to make you forget things almost instantly by switching the subject. Focus is very difficult. I came across a fascinating quote this week from Carl Jung. It said *thinking is difficult, so most people judge instead.* That's a paraphrase, but do me a favor and think about that for a second. What happens in the culture? What is the corporate left culture excellent at? Reaching the lowest common denominator and then giving them something to judge and hold, whereas the right is always encouraged do some hard work learning policy details. Very few people have time to sit and do the deep dives that it takes to think through the problems we have in the political narrative that divides us. I can't tell you how many times I'm using some piece of software and the company decides to switch a bunch of features and you have to go back and redo and relearn and sometimes reinstall and update and mess around with it for hours. Learning the new way that software is going to operate is the exact same thing that happens in political narrative. We're programed with bad information. It sort of works for us in entertaining little ways and we don't realize we're being manipulated. We think we're participating in something that's going to change the future. And then what happens? We get new programing, updated programing and everyone has to relearn. So there's really not a lot of time to sit and think unless you are somebody who has been fortunate enough to be in a position like myself where I kid you not, I spent at least 14 years daydreaming, not really focusing too much on the things that were spoon fed to me through the media, and by daydreaming and simply looking out the window every day, hour here, hour there with really no purpose, your mind starts to receive information and then process it in ways you didn't know were possible. See, the materialist's world is about keeping you busy, so you can't change it. Sub pop culture is about making you aware of this so that we absolutely do change it because if we don't, it just gets worse than it is right now, so we have to start winning the culture. And one of the ways that we're going to win the culture is when we get wise to the idea that we must give people something to judge instead of think about. So how can we on the right achieve this? We're always being suckered into making people judge the temporary when we really want them to judge the big picture. The big picture is where the audience on the left have a reality communicated to them, and the little picture is the little gulag that they have the right held in because we don't ever ask people to or give them something real to judge. Donald

Trump was taken down by the judgment of the people. And so our reaction to that is, *Oh, that's how it works? OK, then let's get them to judge Joe Biden.* Well, nobody wants to do that because once they've committed to something and they've made a judgment, they're very hard to pull away because their judgment is really inspired by layers and layers and layers of manipulation, false information, heartfelt heartstring pulling narratives that are all sliding them in this direction that is away from getting to know the details of how things work. So we have to get into the judgment business. You know in the Bible that it says Jesus will come back to judge the living and the dead. It doesn't say He's going to come back and consider, it doesn't say He's going to come back and think about it for a long time, it says He is going to judge. So this truth about the human animal, this truth about the human spirit is manipulated and used to the advantage of the left. Independent artists are the only ones who are going to be able to put up something clearly juxtaposed to the left that can then be judged, and that judgment has to be against the entire narrative at first. The big picture, not just one offs. When I tell you that all politics is narrative, I truly mean it. And it was proven again when the truck carrying lab monkeys crashed in Pennsylvania that was almost instantly drawn as a comparison to the feature film "Outbreak." This is not an accident, it's intentional. The people who own all of the stories and the intellectual property that has been gobbled up and swallowed by the handful of corporations that run our culture, look at those stories as a toolbox of ways they can harass, frighten, terrify, cultivate, push you around, make you react instead of judge. Look at the life this story has had. Every story is designed to take up about a week or two of your time focused on that instead of something that matters to you. And so a concerned citizen who witnessed the crash helped some of the monkeys that fell out of their cages and got away. And now she's got pink eye and she's got some mystery illness too. And having that story in the news triggers people to remember, *Oh, this is just like outbreak. How scary. What's next?*

Monkeypox! It came months later and served the same time wasting purpose as the crash story. In fact the crash made the monkeypox fear that much more believable. Your mind will fill in the blanks over spelling errors, and your mind will also fill in the blanks when it comes to narrative and the folks who run the media know this. Your imagination will fill in the blanks and say, *holy shit we're all going to die. This is the next disease that will kill us all,* when none of that is going to happen. It's not going to happen, but you can be made to believe it will happen because we've already had the backdrop well established and ingrained in our heads for two years. So think about this—if we ran the movie business, if we ran television, if we owned every story you've ever seen under the sun and we wanted to mess with the public because only a handful of us had our hands in this box of stories and the power to distribute them, think of all the wonderful ways we could turn this culture into a positive thing instead of a chronic panic attack. We have the foundational stories to do that. We have the great moments in the great films and television that everybody remembers as peaceful and uniting. And those comparisons are never made in real life because they don't agitate and they don't increase your ability to get angry and click and share. You know the way that Red was helped by Andy Dufresne in The Shawshank Redemption is a beautiful friendship and one that should be referenced any time there's something good that happens. Where two people in a bad situation help each other get out of it. And what a beautiful movie that is, because of the friendship of those two characters, Andy Dufresne and Red. That's what I'm talking about. To take this journey into the culture requires us to throw water on everything that's inflammatory. Everything that agitates. We will get back to a place where we can raise the roof and have fun, but we have to readjust for a long season. The game table, we have to turn it around, we have to track in another direction and we can't let it be run by an algorithm because an algorithm will know when you've had enough and it will suddenly populate your feeds on Facebook, on Twitter, on whatever social network you're on with things that are going to erase that agitation temporarily so it can have window to change the subject. Soon you have something else put in front of you to get mad about and the cycle begins anew. And then there's the deliberate pictures, the deliberate memes that populate social media at all the right times Videos of kids in the hood helping out some old white lady. Those are wonderful, amazing little stories, but they're being operated by a computer system. They're not being run by us, they're not being reiterated by us. People say *I like that, I love that,* but then they spend all their time talking about human darkness. And so it increases the darkness. Perception is reality. The goal is always to keep your perception focused on what's best for the system, not what's best for you. The system could care less about you, but it needs the people who operate it, and it takes care of the people who operate it up to a point, then it eats them alive as well.

We really do have a long journey ahead of us, but I feel that it's truly beginning now. I feel that people are starting to see the con and they're really starting to understand the importance of—and I know this sounds strange—ignoring the bad things. Unless it happens to you personally, you must ignore it in the news. Go help somebody locally. Go to a food shelter pantry. Donate clothes to goodwill. All those things are 1000 times more helpful to your common neighbor and your fellow man than any of these little stories that we share on social media that have the shelf life of about two minutes before they're replaced with something worse. Social media is not going away. It is the way we all connect now. It's the way I keep in touch with so many people that I probably would have never kept in touch with. And I like it. I enjoy it. So this playing field doesn't go anywhere, but it is programable by us. Don't let anyone tell you different. It's programable by us and once you realize what you click on tells the algorithm what to give you more of or what to give you less of or what you post tells the algorithm to ban you or promote you, you will understand the danger of reactions. And we all know we're being listened to. If you talk about how much you like Yahtzee, suddenly you'll get ads for Yahtzee Games on your social media feeds. That's part of advertising that's not going to go away either. And it also hears you when you say all your political stuff, so stop saying it. It also hears when you talk about how you don't trust the government, so stop saying it, believe it, keep it inside your heart and come up with a code language so that you kind of can have a look between like minded friends that says, *yeah, we don't trust the system*—but we don't have to say it because the system needs to know nothing that you're thinking. It needs to know what you want it to know so that it will react to you in a positive way. Reprogram the system with your clicks. Reprogram the system with what you share. Make those attempts to distract and make us react useless and futile for the system. Take those Pundicrat accounts that are constantly dragging you by the nose to dumpster fires and saying, *Look at this insanity!*—and don't look at it anymore. It's burning and it's on fire, and you don't need to stare at it. You need to turn around, look across the street, see your neighbor, see your friends and say, *How are you doing? Do you need anything?* And in doing so, build these little bridges between ourselves because we're not going to go over the media and build a big giant bridge. We can't go one on one with the system. We have to build the bridge that we can build, and that's with your neighbor and the people you meet every day in real life. Keep that thought in your mind. How many bridges can I build today that bring more unity to me and the people around me because we're all running around like scattered nodes on a system that is corrupted by a virus and we really have to get rid of it, and it takes understanding that the little tiny wins are available and they quickly build up. So stop letting people prevent you from going for the little wins. When really you could fill your basket with them much faster than you can fill it with the fool's gold that the system pretends to offer you.

FOOT ON THE GAS

Every day that goes by, every moment of the news cycle continues to prove my point louder and louder that there is no power without culture, that all politicians in the modern age really do exist downstream from art, history and culture created by historically free people, but in recent times has evolved into total corporatized culture. The system can establish what it wants to make a reality in the people through culture, and then they create the policy afterwards. You see it clear as day. You see exactly what's going on, and now that the world is shifting into a war narrative, it becomes so much more important that we do this work and abandon fond memories of yesterday's reality because it's never coming back. They/Them the world governments did pull off the Great Reset, but we were forced participants in it and we have a say going forward. We maximize our impact on the new narrative that is emerging by becoming an artist driven right wing movement. I think most of us alive remember a time before politics ruined everything but for some people, for a certain generation of people, that's not the case. We do know a time when culture felt unifying and fun and American culture was celebrated and we weren't harassed by government officials trying to divide us to maintain their power. We can bring that back and it's going to be even more fun because the dream of going and making the twenty million dollar payoff in show business is over. But having fun, making a great podcast (I enjoy making the SubPopCult podcast) is a demonstration of time well spent. So is writing independent books that tell a different story. Getting together with your friends and starting a band is time well spent. All the political distractions are a competition for your time. Ask yourself are you spending your time in a way that's going to solve our problems and bring order to chaos? Or are you spending your time contributing to the madness and the chaos? I've been appealing to you since 2020 about the importance of departing from the system, and what I'm talking about is getting you going into the arena of, to put it in plain English, having a great time with your freedoms. Weed is legal just about everywhere now. People can drink or they can smoke marijuana. There's the ability to create independent content and put it out into the world for all to see. Just imagine your day is a little different than in the past when you were conditioned to hit your nose to the grindstone and then be spoon fed a movie that everyone goes to see and then you are spoon fed an opinion on the nightly news. It's totally different now. You might do some hybrid version of your job. You might have two or three different jobs. Then you go and you get your libation of choice, or you get a little bag of weed. You download some independent film made by a nobody and you kick back and watch it and you start telling your friends about it, and then they tell their friends and things just kind of organically grow that way. But you must do it intentionally and with focus to avoid the glittering offerings of the corporate system. Makes these adjustments and you're really going to change the dynamic of what it feels like to be an American in the year 2023 and beyond.

There's another reason the culture is dominated by the left, besides having all of their hands close to the levers of cultural power, manipulating it, kicking out conservatives, all that stuff. It's because of an organization called the Creative Coalition. It was started in 1980 by a few Hollywood actors and talented people that recognize the importance of culture, and it still exists to this day but it is basically a lobbyist for left wing cultural interests. And there's nobody putting pressure on the right to do this because what we do is we fall in line with the right wing politicians and their stories and fake punditry. And right before every presidential election, we'll all be saying we must stand with Israel and its important relationship with America. But we know it's the culture that creates the political power now and we can stand with Israel (we can stand with whoever we want) but we also have to stand with our own American melting pot culture first, otherwise, we're not standing on anything and that has been proven over and over and over again. I'm so sick of it. Aren't you sick of it? The conservative base is not standing on anything. There's nothing behind anything a Republican says other than outrage. Meanwhile the left is so big it has the whole field covered. They can create outrage and they can create culture. And then politicians on both sides are forced step up and say, *look, here's why I have to do this thing. It's what the people want. It's what they do. It's how they live.* This power is not that complicated. It really originates in the culture. That is our slogan going forward. We need to answer with some originality, while also taking a little bit from their playbook from the 1960s, because really, if you think about it, we've been forced to celebrate and worship the 1960s for as long as most of us have been alive. Year after year, there'll be a period where news and entertainment networks present the 1960s as a look back at history, always waxing nostalgic about everything that happened in that time. And when you realize that everybody in power is still working off that same script, you can begin to understand why it's important to tear down the culture of the 1960s and replace it with our own. What I propose, what I'd like to see if I had a magic wand, is that we take the culture of the 1960s and throw it in the garbage can. We replace it with the culture of the 1980s, the fun, pro-American Reagan baby culture that Dave Chappelle talked about on his Comedy Central show. We replace it with that, and we force people for the next 50 years to celebrate all the great unity and pro-American positivity and destruction of Communism that was part of 1980s culture. Let's keep that for the next 50 years and just ram it down everyone's throat until they get bored with us and then someone comes along and figures out a way to undo it and start a new movement. The 1960s propels the left but is boring now. It's gone to its logical conclusion, which is total absurdity. That's why every weird little thing is embraced, because they know it's better to have people paying attention to you than ignoring you. They do not want to be ignored. It's the end of power in media. We have that power. We can ignore them. So, let's start and let's just change what we do with our time until the system is brought to heel. Work on your book. Start that band. Learn filmmaking. Finish that film. All these little things that you do, they help the economy, too, because the creator economy is about small little transactions everywhere, whether it's me downloading a clip or some audio that I'm licensing or someone else going to the store and buying a camera, all this stuff doesn't feed-back directly into Hollywood. The only thing that feeds-back into Hollywood is when you put your eyes on the screen and watch and devour and consume everything they make, and you ignore the original independent voices of the artists in your own country. If we spend our time trying to undo the addiction, I promise you that will be time well spent. You'll make way more memories, you'll have way more laughs, you'll have way more fun just doing this stuff. So even if you feel assaulted by the culture that the left jams down everyone's throat and eyes and ears and whatever orifice they can get in with their culture, then take joy in pushing back on that, even in the smallest way because it is rewarding. You can close your door at the end of the night when the sun's going down. You can take that last look at the sunset, and you can say, you know, I wasn't a sucker for all the politicized corporate stuff. Today I watched two totally weird Avant Garde indie films: one from a guy in Kansas and another from a girl in Brooklyn. And I downloaded this book from as cool indie sci fi writer I have never heard of before.

I'm glad to be at the front of the new culture train asking you to come with me, because we will answer the Creative Coalition with Sub Pop Culture. I will take this organization that I'm slowly, slowly, patiently growing, and I will one day convert it into a 501c3 charitable org and get a law firm to represent it and use that law firm and basically put pressure on every elected Republican and policymaker to create a co-equal side of culture. We're not going to be dominated by one sided culture in this country, but we don't need to fracture into two economies to solve the problem. We must start working towards unity and accepting each other for all of our differences and start to turn the fire back on and get that melting pot going so we can put pressure on people to unify America. The next move is to start inching closer and closer and closer to the power of culture exactly like the left did. Eventually we will start to make art that affects the entire culture by cultivating in the people qualities that are good for unity. But this is going to take stubborn artists who are not easily persuaded by a buyout and a blowjob. Yeah, I know. That's blunt, but that's what it is. Sex and money. Everybody's got a price. But we must have no price right now because if the future is all about information, it's critical that free American people create and distribute and receive from one another the information of their life and what it's like, because it's the only place to get authentic information about the world we live in. It's pressure cooker time. Newly elected Republicans if you can't deliver on culture based legislation, it starts to create opportunities for more leftist culture to be created in this country by one political party and its ownership of the entire narrative. If you can't prioritize getting us out of this gulag, we will have to replace you. I don't think that we should let you run on how you stand with a foreign nation or what your foreign policy is going to be. We ought to demand that you deliver to us the fair opportunities that we should have to create a co-equal voice in this country. Being drowned out and marginalized and pushed aside only benefits the people that you're in lockstep with. And we know that. So, we'll make sure to pay attention from now on and find people who will get us what we want. Because ultimately, that's what it's about. Foreign nations come in and they get out of you what they want for their nation. People deliver large amounts of money to you and they get out of you legislation that's favorable to their business. What do you give We the People other than bullshit talking points, trickle down nonsense, legends of the past, fanning the flames of masculinity and alpha male absurdity and using the left's ridiculous culture in the same way, practically. But you're never doing anything to fix the problem, and that must end. So, we're going to organize. We're going to organize around an artistic movement. And very slowly we're going to start to put pressure on you, and that pressure is going to get hot, and that hot pressure is going to either make you run away from the scene because you can't deliver, or you're going to roll up your sleeves to do what's right. You're going to help us start cooking a new culture in this country that is based on Liberty, freedom and most importantly, the right to free speech. I don't want reactions about free speech anymore. I want action creating culture that enables it and edifies it and keeps it alive in the hearts and minds of all the people. Because that's what happens when culture is what's teaching history and how the world works as you internalize the moments. It's a sophisticated art form that involves a lot of psychology. Let's use that to cultivate the American culture that we know and love that is hidden beneath the corporate culture. I don't know about you, but I'm done with the Republican Party and I'm not a Democrat, but I'm done with the Republican Party until they prioritize an independent American culture.

WIELDING THE SIMULACRUM

"*The simulacrum is true. Abstraction today is no longer that of the map, the double, the mirror or the concept. Simulation is no longer that of a territory, a referential being or a substance. It is the generation by models of a real without origin or reality. It is hyper real.*" - *Jean Baudrillard*

When I was nominated for an Academy Award, I was unaware that hyperreality had replaced reality and it all revolved around simulacrums. The Webster's Dictionary definition of simulacrum is *an image or representation of someone or something, an unsatisfactory imitation or substitute.* That's what Simulacrum means. But the definition given by French sociologist, philosopher and cultural theorist Jean Baudrillard goes like this "*The simulacrum is never what hides the truth. It is the truth that hides the fact that there is none. The simulacrum is true.*" And then in the book, this quote definition is credited to the book of Ecclesiastes yet it never appears there. The lesson here is that what you see, hear or read is what you accept as the truth. 99% of the time. And I was never nominated for an Academy Award but many of you believed it when you read it. Let's explore and try to get an understanding between us indie artists of how the simulacrum is wielded by the media and the government to create these false realities that we fall into and accept, primarily because people are too busy to stop and think and dig through all the layers, because we've been buried over time by so many that it's almost impossible to see past this one ultra-powerful trick. We'll look at how a weaponized cultural simulacrum plays into season two of the famous popular television series Yellowstone but first, let me explain what I mean by wielding a simulacrum.

The simulacrum and the simulation run on perception is reality. Smoke and mirrors are tools to pull off the trick, but the simulacrum is how it is delivered into your mind. A simulacrum is the sword of deception. The sword of deception is the simulacrum that you believe on the surface what it' telling you and you accept what it's saying as truth. Something completely nonexistent that doesn't originate from anything real can be made to seem as if it has been real since the beginning of time. This is a very powerful society shaping tool that is used against We the People, and it should never be used against us because we don't even know what it is or how it works but we're going to change that with this chapter. The clearest example of how the simulacrum works in politics is how we all know that no matter what side of the political spectrum we're on, what the person or the party we're supporting is up to and what they do-- their big agenda that people vote for in presidential elections creates the ability for the winning administration to create policy, which is always going to produce results, good or bad. And when somebody gets elected that you really dislike, like when you didn't vote for Obama, but he became the president and then he did a bunch of things that became policies, the whole time he was blaming George Bush for his failures. And he kept blaming and he kept blaming. It was all what George

Bush did. That's the simulacrum. He repeated it enough and stuck to that talking point long enough and people begin to absolutely believe it. So, in many ways, wielding the simulacrum by Obama was one of the very first deep cuts put into the fabric of this nation. Because never has somebody so long and so passionately attacked their predecessor to the point where it was if, *hey, there's nothing I can do here, the guy before me ruined everything and so we've got to start from zero.* That was a very sophisticated wielding of the simulacrum. And I understand that every administration that comes to power does lay some blame on the previous administration, but not for eight years, not for the entirety of a new administration. That's why it was a deep cut. Another way the simulacrum waits to be used by those who know how, is that some of the Trump policies produced good results. Some of the things that Republicans had achieved produced positive results. And then in social media and just talking among people, there's an instant frustration when Joe Biden stands up and takes credit for somebody else's work. This is also a tradition in politics because remember, the game of government and media is to keep power away from We the People while pretending it's ours. So a guy like Biden stands up to the podium and he says, *Thanks to my work getting the vaccines out the American people in record time, thanks to my presidential powers, thanks to my executive orders, we've saved millions of lives.* He takes the credit for something that was initiated and began in the Trump administration. That's the simulacrum. It's being wielded again in a way that only the bully pulpit can broadcast as the most heard voice in American politics. It doesn't even matter what truly happened. It doesn't even matter who rolled out the vaccine in record time, what matters is who said they did it and <u>when</u> they say it. And that's a big part of how this narrative driven power game works. If you stop and think about what happens every time a

politician goes out and he takes credit for what somebody else did, the true believers on either side will spend
days and days pointing and saying, *That's a lie. That's a
lie.* But most people are not true believers. Most people
are just casual observers. Those casual observers believe
what they hear when they hear it. When the left has a
problem in the economy and then it begins to fix that
problem, it doesn't matter how much the right pointed
to their work and said it's the left's fault, and no matter
how much the base knows, it's left's fault. All that matters to the casual observers is when the fix starts to begin, when the gas prices start to go down, the casual
observers will believe whatever they're told about how it
got there. And then they'll reiterate it to those around
them with a typical conversation going like this. *"Oh.
Did you see gas is $3.99 per gallon today? It's down quite
a bit and it happened fast. Oh, yeah, Biden went and
shook up the Saudi leader and he got him to release more
barrels of oil. I know those crazy right wingers say he's
done, but he's a good president if ya ask me."* That's how
it goes--not in your mind and not in my mind, but in
the mind of casual observers who are the direct target of
all political narrative. The direct target of the simulacrum.

Elon Musk is also a master of wielding the simulacrum. Think about his Boring company and the
videos that you saw of flame throwers. You're not seeing
flame throwers for sale everywhere despite the fact that
he made a few. It's not like a widespread product available at Home Depot but it created a perception in your
mind of this scientific genius billionaire guy who is a lot
like Tony Stark in many ways. That's wielding the simulacrum to create an image though perception. The flame
throwers are just really cool props. How about the sophisticated videos of what cars and busses will do in
cities when they pull over and they enter the hyper
tunnel that he's advocating for, claiming they'll go from

New York to Philadelphia in 15 minutes. There's no ground broken on any of that, but it creates an image in your mind that it's going to happen one day, so they're already in planting the future in your mind in many ways. They're doing it because they failed us and they dropped the ball, the system failed us and now China's way ahead of the United States in building these sophisticated new technologies quicker, faster, (but not better) so we get the simulacrum wielded at us, which is a giant deception. And we don't get anything to back it up other than the loss of more individual liberty. That's not a good price to pay for being deceived.

Now let's talk about a much deeper level of simulacrum, the real deep stuff that I'm pleased to share with you that I can explain in great detail. When I talk about the narrative and how the narrative is the plot beneath the plot, the nudge, the little moments, in television shows and commercials that paint pictures or edify political talking points, like the most obvious little tiny nudge that you and I can recognize when you deliberately see an interracial couple in a commercial for example. Advertisers are appealing to interracial couples. I'm in an interracial marriage and those advertisers are trying to appeal to me, but they're also creating a false reality that makes it seem like everybody is in an interracial marriage and this also creates an passive acceptance that white people must be going away, that there's no more white people. All this does is enables the real assholes in the political narrative game to use their own little, tiny simulacrums. They take this type of commercial and then use it as an example of how they're trying to eradicate white people. So it's a very dangerous tool because the person who wields it, the individuals, the association, the system, the political gestapo, whatever you want to call it, that wields the simulacrum just by the default of using it, they make it possible for others to use too because there's one billion voices to be heard online, all telling you what they think something means. And I understand the irony of me writing that right now in a book where I'm trying to tell you what this stuff means, but I'm going somewhere with this, specifically to the television series Yellowstone. Yellowstone is an excellent TV series on the Paramount Plus Network. (I've been watching it on Peacock.) The drama revolves around the Dutton family, which represent a very classic, you could say, conservative values family that uses weapons and violence to defend their private land. But the problem is not that they have this land by stealing it from Native Americans or that they defend it, but that the Dutton's are mostly ruthless, evil people. And they will do anything to hold on to their land. This is the drama. The point I'm making here is that they're not great people, the Dutton's, they're bad people, but they're the heroes of the show and are used to attract a conservative audience. As the seasons goes on its a fine show where characters make mistakes and go through life, paying the price for those mistakes. But where the show takes a turn and where it connects to our modern political era and where we're going in the 2024 election is found at the end of season two. Everybody who attacks the ranch either gets killed or offed or severely beaten or shot and pushed over a cliff to never be seen again. And the show became very popular. When a show becomes popular. The culture sharks who are all persuasion through narrative experts, force their involvement and use it to wield the simulacrum on behalf of the system. We all know that a big part of the Democrat's talking points is white supremacy or what they call homegrown right wing terrorist extremism, whatever they're calling it, it pretends to be one thing, but is basically a description of people who want to have their guns and not have the government powerful enough to stop them from owning weapons and having the individual liberty and the freedom to defend themselves and live freely. The

Gadsden flag is a big part of this as is *Don't tread on me.*
These are all touchstones that we know is the characterization by the media of people they consider unsavory
and dangerous, more dangerous than a terrorist in the
Middle East, more dangerous than, you know, rampant
crime in Chicago. *These right wingers are the most dangerous people walking the face of earth and you will believe
it or else! These white power, white supremacists, racist,
fascist, gun loving nuts are dangerous.* Now, here's the
spoiler (if you don't want to know what happens in the
later episodes of season two, stop reading this chapter)
because I have to talk about how this episode at the end
of season two became the setup to a simulacrum to be
wielded in the road to 2024 by Democrats. Here's what
happens: Kevin Costner is the patriarch of the family,
and he has a grandson who is kidnaped by some people
who want to get back at Costner's character and his
family. What they do is show the kidnapped kid was
taken by the white supremacists. White supremacists
come out nowhere, never to be seen in this series until
all of a sudden, out of left field, literally, there's white
supremacists the town over, and that's where his
grandson is. The episode is dramatic. The Dutton's get
together his family and also gets together with the Native Americans he fought for most of the first two seasons and they work together as a team to go in and kill
and destroy these white supremacists and get that
grandkid back. (Who has a Native American mother)
When they bust into the home where these people are,
there's all the things you would expect on display.
There's the Gadsden flag with a bald-headed white guy
sitting there looking ferociously at camera, filled with
hate and rage. Costner asks him, *Where is my grandson?*
The skin head blows his own head off. They end up
pushing through the home and finding the grandkid
hiding in the bathtub, terrified, screaming, and his head
is completely shaved. He is now a skinhead in the mak-

ing. They were going to turn him into a Neo Nazi. Now, if you're paying attention, you understand that that scene, that episode of that popular show which gained an audience and got the eyes of casual observers who lean right, watched a climatic episode that wielded the simulacrum and created a real world inception in their mind, a reality in their mind of the white supremacist as the most dangerous, ruthless character that should be the center of why we need more government power and why we need to take your guns away. That's exactly what this message is, delivered through this episode. That's why it was inserted into the show because it just feels so completely forced compared to everything else you've seen in the show so far. Next, what will happen is in 2024, politicians on the left will all run on this. They will all say we need to curb right wing extremism. They'll talk about, reiterate and draw this conversation back to January 6th, to the "insurrection" and the whole narrative that they've set up and seeded over there matches with this simulacrum, which now exists in the back of the mind of television audiences as not an episode in a show, but as a distant, foggy memory of something that is real in the real world not far from their home. And the show is just giving you a glimpse. That's the simulacrum. It existed in the show so now it's real in their minds. I know there's white supremacists in this world. I know there's Neo Nazis in this world and all kinds of haters and KKK types. We're all aware of it, but 99.9% of all people have never seen, met, or ever encountered somebody with that level of hate and violence in their heart. And that's just a fact. But the simulacrum is always true to the casual observer. Try this game--see if you can identify a simulacrum every time you see it. It's any time you're told some sensational fact or shown some piece of evidence or shown some video speculation. If it isn't totally true and provable with your own eyes in the real world, then it most likely doesn't exist as advertised.

The bottom line is we are living in a simulation. The simulation is the political and social narrative of our time that drives government policy. Our real world is physical and right before us every day in broad daylight, but the simulation exists in the passive hive mind, made possible by networked computers and devices working as extensions for human conditioning, reiterated through culture. Everyone sees everything for exactly what it is, but also for what they imagine it is.

Both are true.

NUANCE

Nuance is not a bad word. Nuance is a required quality that we must embrace so that we can get over the political divisions and repair our family relationships and our local communities. Because if you think about it, when you deal with people one on one, you are nuanced in real life. Very few people act as uptight and sure of themselves and one sided in real life as they do on social media. We have to bring that nuance of the real world into our online world so that we can overcome these narratives that really require you to be the opposite of nuanced to participate in the show. They/Them the Gov/Media complex need you to be so certain of what you believe in or what you've been told to believe in, that you can be manipulated and pitted against the other guy. Resisting being pitted against the other guy is the key factor that must always be running through your heart. I know this doesn't make sense. Sometimes when I say these things, it's wrongly inter-preted as *We shouldn't get mad at the left's treatment of the right. We shouldn't fight about politics.* That's not what I'm saying at all. We must take a nuanced approach instead. Nuance is not a voice that is ever heard from the right and when one tires to be nuanced the system has them surrounded by storytelling against this powerful tool. The left gets to have its crazies and its large number of people turned on and activated to answer much louder and harass in a much louder voice against the entire right and it keeps us in a little gulag. What the right must do to overcome that is become nuanced. Nuance is very important, so let's talk about it a little bit because it is the path to personal freedom and liberty and peace of mind so that you can move forward and not be somebody's chess piece in a game where you make no money, but you lose power and permanently spend your life as a pawn to the system. It doesn't need to be this way.

Lawyers will tell you that law is open to interpretation. And if you think about it, lawyers who are successful are very good at tabling their argument using nuance and bringing people to their side of interpretation. Slight differences in opinion are easier to tolerate than dramatic hard cuts in opinion. When somebody has a nuanced approach, they understand that in the back and forth where they're talking to somebody and maybe trying to change their mind about a subject to stand with your flag planted in the ground that says *My way or the highway* just makes people run further and further and further from what you're trying to tell them, what you're trying to communicate, what you're trying to share. It's a big giant turnoff. That's why you're inspired to do this all the time by paid professionals, because they make their money by getting you to be brash and lacking any nuance. But really, if you're nuanced, you can understand the value of small gains. Maybe the person you're trying to reach is far from you politically, socially, whatever. They're just very far from you. But a nuanced approach might bring them a little bit closer and then later a little bit closer again. And soon you're talking face to face and you're finding some common ground and peace. That's the spot that we must get to on the political right through culture and nuance so that we can have that intimate mind changing conversations and then start to tell them the things that you really believe and why. It's all about timing with the political narrative. The right puts the cart before the horse all the time. The left understands this, so they make it possible for us to put the cart before the horse and make it seem like we're making progress. There's no progress. Nuance is the key. Nuance will allow you to look at videos and the things that politicians say while not falling for another storytelling effort by the left and right, working together to make you think that there's this big, awesome power taking your freedom away, taking your liberty away. They juxtapose that lie with Biden's disinformation ministry and it feels true to most people. The left takes its cue from the top, and its mission is to prevent basic, normal American people from organizing and gathering power together and having a voice. We don't need to shout our desired policies at the left. What you really want to do is get a nuanced response instead of *You're a Bible thumper and I hate you,* or *You're an atheist and I hate you because you're Satanic.* That that's the dumb, unnuanced territory that you can fall into and you're so much better than that. Your mind is better than that. Your capability is vast compared to that small mindedness which says, *I got to get one over on you* or *I'm right and you're wrong again.* It is all possible due to a lack of nuance. It's really a dangerous situation to not embrace it. So let's embrace nuance. Let's embrace the small wins. Let's go for the little, tiny, incremental moments that draw people closer to our side and closer to our reality. Look, it's all teed up and it's really easy to do because the system is corrupt, and everybody knows it. But you get distracted from focusing on that corruption in a way that makes it impossible for you to understand it. Instead, you focus on it as a fire that must be put out by your louder and louder and louder reaction to the corruption. That's not how we put the fires out. The fire gets put out person by person, one at a time with a little bit of nuance. That's the thing that we're being inspired on the right to not embrace. If we embrace it and we add it to our toolbox of understanding how the system works, understanding that storytelling drives reality, that storytelling has a beginning, a middle and an end with a conflict--if you understand those basic realities, you can start to unpack every media story and then make them work for your own means.

Whether you exist on the far left or the far right, the only thing both of those positions do is keep us all far from power. It's designed that way because on both extremes, nuance disappears. That's called sophisticated con job 101. When you are made to look like it's your fault for what was taken from you and was rightfully yours in the first place—I'm talking about the American culture that belongs to the American people who create it, not the corporations who distribute it—it's almost like we're at a point with culture where movie theaters were a long time ago the drive in theater was secondary and it didn't get the films that were in the movies because the studios owned the movie theaters and they kept that loop closed. Well, now most information distribution channels are owned, and the loop is still closed. You're no longer an artist in this country or a creator that puts things out and they organically grow and then corporations catch on. Instead, it's the opposite. Corporations manufacture grassroots movements that are fake, put product out, create movements, close them down, repeat, wash, rinse, repeatedly, all the way to the bank. So no more extreme right, no more extreme left. It's time to really go to the center. Every time we have an election, the right wing Punditcrats and the leftist pundits are the people on cable TV that are part of that class where they're getting paid a nice living to mess with our power, our unity. The Pundicrats simply want to be the cable news pundits one day. So these folks work really hard to radicalize as many people in each side as they can, so that when it comes to election time, everybody is on fire. Nobody knows what time it is. Nobody can see straight. And then we believe anything is a relief. We'll stand with whoever can make it stop. We will stand with a donkey. We'll stand with an elephant. We'll stand with Israel. We'll stand with Iran. You can have this country divided up however you want when the people follow that divisive, extreme storytelling without nuance or question. But if we demand nuance and we practice nuance ourselves, that won't be so possible anymore. They won't be able to bastardize the middle because the middle is precisely where you live. You don't live in an extreme. You live in the middle. You don't walk out your door with a hammer in one hand and every person that you disagree with gets hammered by it. That's just not what you do, so don't do it online. It doesn't help you. It's not a reflection of who you are. It just propagates the divide that gets many people more and more radicalized and uncivilized. You can set your clock to it the closer we get to an election.

The system is having a harder time now and I'm positive I've had an impact at this point because people who are on the right are grifters, so they're always searching for what the next grift is. I've set the SubPop-Cult message up to be something that is un-griftable, because by preaching this message and copying and reiterating what I say, you help lead us all to the better place. So that's what needs to be done. No more extremism. Defend the center. Don't let anybody tell you that you can't exist there because that's where nuance is found and therefore so is the ability to win power. And nuance is what we are missing. Let's be nuanced in our approach to politics. We're always talking about the need to have a detailed conversation in a back and forth, but the left has always put their hands up and say, no. That's them saying, *you cannot be nuanced*. Reject that. Be totally nuanced in every situation. But all of us must do it. If we can have a chorus of nuanced, reasonable people we will be unstoppable because everything they/them says will not add up to anything that We the People see. They'll have to start putting fake character actors out there to pretend to be crazed right wingers, which they already do. And our side also puts out fake versions of leftists to keep the divide going. But let's outsmart them this time. Let's put an end to it for a cycle until we can reestablish a fair game, a fair playing field. As I told you in the past, I have long operated in the game of political theater, which is a lot of fun when you are operating under the impression that it's basically a fair game, going back and forth, fighting over things until power changes hands—but we've seen power get rapidly consolidated instead. Therefore, we have to all take a collective six to eight year pause from letting the system do that to us so that we can reclaim our power, put the government in its place. Think about nuance as you go about your week and see people in real life. Consider what you're doing in public and then reflect on how it is compared to your online persona and understand that it does have an impact on the political outcomes that we're all sick and tired of living through. Let's put an end to that in this era, and let's restore American culture through one positive reiteration at a time.

ABOUT THE AUTHOR

Michael McGruther is an actor, screenwriter, director, author, publisher, and founder of the SubPopCult grassroots artists movement. He has worked in the entertainment industry for 30 years, first in TV commercials and small roles in films before his professional screenwriting career began with the original screenplay Tigerland, (directed by Joel Schumacher and starring Colin Farrell in his feature film debut) The Puddle Club is the first book released under his publishing imprint Hosel & Ferrule Books and was named one the Best Indie Books of the Year by Kirkus Reviews in 2018. He resides in the Philadelphia suburbs where the cornfields meet cannabis shops.

ALSO BY MICHAEL MCGRUTHER

THE PUDDLE CLUB

A fine teaching tool that offers advice for getting through a golf game—and through life.

-Kirkus Reviews

CRISIS MOON

The US discovers China operates a secret hidden base on the Moon and the only quick option is to partner with an anti-government private sector spaceship entrepreneur to get boots on the ground before the highest ground is lost forever.

OMIM

An intriguing but intensely violent SF tale.

-Kirkus Reviews